To M:

Thank you [...] means the world to me. Remember, family first... always

Honoring Our Fathers

HONORING OUR FATHERS

Celebrating a Man's Role in
His Family and Community

Anthony Laws

BROWN BOOKS
PUBLISHING GROUP

FATHERS HONORING OUR

Manufactured in the United States of America.

For information, please contact:

Brown Books Publishing Group
16200 North Dallas Parkway, Suite 170
Dallas, Texas 75248
www.brownbooks.com
972-381-0009

A New Era in Publishing™

ISBN-13: 978-1-934812-47-1
ISBN-10: 1-934812-47-1

LCCN: 2009928379

anthonyplaws@yahoo.com

DEDICATION

To my father, William Arthur Laws, Sr.

ACKNOWLEDGMENTS

————————⬤————————

I feel really strongly about the story I have to tell. A lot of it has to do with the legacy of a man and how his children and other people will remember him. Many people make celebrity a reason for remembering people. Others find role models in actors, athletes, and politicians. I often wonder how many men, especially men my age, can find a role model in their father.

My father is my role model and the only one I have ever needed. Dad has always conducted himself in an honorable manner and his selfless deeds, wise decisions, and confident demeanor reflect his inner strength and integrity. It is not something he is conscious of; it is just in him. My dad is the most humble man I have ever known and doesn't like to be the center of attention. He sits back and observes what is happening in his surroundings, as he is a keen observer.

Pops is an educated man, but he is also street smart. He is eloquent in his speech and manner, but he is a fierce warrior when the situation warrants it. He is an honest, loving man, filled with pride and confidence. He is a faithful believer in the Supreme presence of good. Further, with the exception of his time spent in the Vietnam War and the times he was away training in the military, I saw my father every day.

My father and my mother raised ten healthy, happy children, and our lives have been blessed. At this time, I'd like to thank my brothers and sisters for their assistance in this endeavor. You will also read their thoughts about our father.

This book is intended to help others recall and remember who the real role models, for living and being, were and are intended to be. It is an account filled with pride, laughter, learning, and loving, and I hope that it will have an impact on someone's life.

After you have read of my childhood under the guidance of my father, I would like to hear from you, recalling your thoughts and feelings about your father. There have to be other men and women who feel about their fathers the way my siblings and I do about ours. I would like to continue to publish volumes of letters and stories about the men we grew up loving and looking to for guidance. I will edit the stories and letters for sentence structure and punctuation and publish them so we don't forget how good men live their lives. Reach out to me at anthonyplaws@yahoo.com.

This book celebrates my father and the legacy of his fathers before him. It is an honor to present it to you.

My father's son,
Anthony

TABLE OF CONTENTS

PROLOGUE

C ompton Camp Laws, born into American slavery in or around the year 1825, begat a son named George in 1858. George Laws begat a son on September 10, 1885 named Otis Laws (my grandfather). Otis Laws begat a son on March 11, 1925, named William A. Laws (my father). William Arthur Laws begat a son on September 1, 1958, named Anthony Paul Laws (me). I begat a son on August 6, 1976, named Anthony Paul Laws Jr.

My great-great-grandfather, Compton Camp Laws, had other children. My great-grandfather, George Laws, had other children as well. My grandfather, Otis Laws, had other children, my aunts and uncles, with whom I have interacted regularly throughout my life and whom I love dearly. As mentioned earlier, my father has nine other children in addition to me, and I, too, have another child. My second son's name is Brandon Tyrea Laws.

I am the proud product of a long line of patriarch-led families, dating back to the days of slavery. I have been blessed to sit at the feet of some of the bravest, most intelligent and proud men I have ever known. The blood of all of them runs through my veins and the veins of my sons. My point in delineating my patriarchal family tree is to impress upon everyone that while some men have long been ostracized for not assuming their responsibility as leaders of their families and fathers to their offspring, there are others who shoulder that responsibility gladly, generation after generation. Having heard many of the old stories that are my history, I sit in awe of my ancestral fathers' commitments made and hardships endured that I might thrive in this world!

My mother often related stories she heard as a child about slaves who were beaten because they stood up straight and tall, refusing to cower. For this book, she sat and spoke with me on several occasions about the injustices waged against black men during her childhood, and the lasting ill-effect it has had on some black men today. She becomes extremely passionate thinking about those stories. She holds the America of that time and, in part, the America of today responsible for the pain and angst of many black families.

My father, true to his nature, suggests that the black family's struggle throughout the history of America has been due to ignorance and shame. Initially, America was ignorant of, or did not concern itself with, the long-term damage it inflicted on black people. Ignorance resulted in a lack of care and concern. Later, shame became so deeply a part of the American fabric that efforts to correct injustices toward black people swung like a pendulum back and forth, never stopping on an effective course of enlightening the ignorant and placating the shame felt for the abusive treatment of black people.

In spite of all of the hardships that we've had to endure, I am honored, proud, and thankful for the strength of the men that set the course for me to follow. It is a course that was mapped out by a strong, caring, committed succession of black men. Now, I am honoring our father, and his father, and his father, and his. . . .

SECTION ONE

A FAMILY TREE WITH STRONG ROOTS

My father, William Arthur Laws, Sr. was born on March 11, 1925, *near Bryan, Texas*. Those words are actually written on the birth certificate of one of his children as his birthplace: near Bryan, Texas. He is the son of Otis Glasco and Leugenia Turner Laws, my grandparents. My grandparents had eleven children. Two died at birth. Dad had four brothers but only my Uncle Oscar and Dad are still alive. His eldest brother, Columbus, died at the age of four and his brothers, Aubrey and Bert, have passed in the last year. He had four sisters; three are deceased and one, my Aunt Queen, lives near me, here in Dallas, Texas. Both of my father's parents, my grandparents, are deceased.

Dad lived on a farm out in the country. You know, Country with a capital "C." The farm was eleven miles west of Bryan, Texas, along Highway 21, about two miles east of FM 50. He says that back in the days of his youth, there was a thriving farming community out there. Several hundred black families, several brown families, and a few white families lived, worked, and prospered there.

Visiting the home of my father's childhood when I was young included making trips to the outhouse, the hog pen, the chicken coop, the trash-burning barrel, and the well. I can remember pumping the handle of that well and drawing water to take a bath in the middle of my grandparents' kitchen in a #2 washtub. The water was heated on a wood-burning stove that required someone's effort to keep it filled with wood and to keep the fire burning.

I would get up very early in the morning to try and catch my grandfather exiting the back door of the house heading for the chicken coop. Assisting him as he fed the chickens was a special event for me. Grandpa Otis made this clucking, crooning noise with his mouth that would have the chickens scurrying out of the chicken coop to flurry around his feet as he fed them.

Next, he carried an old slop bucket filled with last evening's leftover supper, to the shed. There, he added dried corn, old fruit and vegetables, chicken bones, and anything else perishable that had not been eaten and could not be salvaged. He would stir this nauseating mixture thoroughly and then walk over to the hog pen and slop the hogs. To this day, I am totally convinced that hogs will eat anything that is put in front of them.

I cherish those times that I spent with my grandfather because that is when I had his undivided attention and he taught me things. I can recall thinking that this man, my Grandpa Otis, was the spitting image of my dad, except that Grandpa was a light-skinned black man and Pops is dark-skinned. My grandfather was part Native American and you could see that in his features. He had high, prominent cheekbones, a small sharp nose and average sized lips. Mama Honey, Dad's mom, was a dark-skinned black woman with a flatter face, a broader nose, and thicker lips than her husband had. When Dad smiled or laughed, I always stared in amazement that he looked so much like his father and mother, at the same time.

By the time I was old enough to know what false teeth were, my grandfather had them. My grandmother, on the other hand, was ninety-eight years old when she died, and at that time she still had all of her natural teeth.

As a young boy, I was fascinated with the simplicity of life in the country. The air smelled cleaner, the sun shone brighter, the sky seemed clearer, and the breeze blew softer. I felt elated to sleep in the bed that my father slept in as a boy.

I remember crossing the watermelon patch from my grandparents' house to the home of my aunt. Along the way, I might step around a coiled snake, spy a darting lizard moving swiftly over the hot, red dirt, or shoot at a horned toad sunning on a rock with my BB gun. As I crossed the watermelon patch, I would stop to crack open a fully ripe watermelon and eat the heart of it. I would leave the rest of that perfectly good melon where it lay on the ground, right out in that hot sun.

I think that it was spiritual, as I look back on it, because I can remember how happy I was. It was during those joyous moments crossing that watermelon patch, filled with happiness at visiting the childhood home of my father—my grandfather's house—that I would become emotionally overwhelmed and cry. Those beautiful moments! Those moments when I knew that I was protected and loved and looked after would fill me with wonder, and I would begin to weep. In those moments, all of my love for both Dad and my Grandpa Otis would well up inside of me, and I would cry unashamedly.

I often would arrive at one destination or another in the community of my relatives with a smile on my face and tears streaming down my cheeks. I remember that I could never explain to anyone "what the matter was" with me. I didn't quite know myself. All I knew was that something was touching me as I walked along the path that my father had walked when he was a boy like me.

I did not realize it then, but I now know that the love and guidance I have tried to provide to my sons originated there. Four previous generations of strong, proud men, my patriarchal bloodline, have infused me with the emotional strength and fortitude to be another strong, proud man and to pass that emotional strength and pride to my sons.

I speak with my dad and see him regularly and have come to count on this constant in my life. It is an expectation that comes from being able to rely on him my entire life. He is constant; he is steady; he is my father—and he is my role model!

Over the course of my life I have referred to my father using different names. As a child, he was my daddy. As I grew older, I called him Dad. He's been Sarge, Pops, Old Man, and Top. And as you will come to understand, he is my rock.

Pops and I have talked about practically everything there is to talk about. I love to hear him tell about his youth, about his life under the guidance of his father. Hearing my father talk about his life on that same farm that I have memories of visiting when I was a child makes me smile. It also makes me realize that my father is a special man.

He recognized something within himself that drove him to seek out his fortune, his life, away from the small-town environment and mentality. He recognized that he was destined to expand his mind and horizons. He wanted something more than the life of a sharecropper. His faith in himself, the strength passed down through generations of strong, proud black men that are the Laws men, the perseverance to endure the hardships of life—all have combined to make the man that is my father.

Dad listened to the radio as a youth and heard the Joe Louis fights. Joe Louis was one of the few black role models for black Americans on a national level. Other than Jesse Owens, there were not too many other black national sports celebrities. There were few black film stars in that day, as well.

There were not many role models for black people to look to for leadership and representation. It was a difficult time. My father did say that some of the black athletes who played in the regional and national Negro Baseball League were quite popular in the various communities. It was a time in America when blacks were not allowed to compete against whites, and the few black national sports icons of the day were still treated as second-class citizens by society and the media.

It was only when they could be used as propaganda images in America's fight against Nazism, and later against communism, that these black icons received any fair and adequate treatment. Jesse Owens was a hero for all Americans when he won gold medals in the '36 Olympics against Hitler's supposedly superior Aryan race, but was still not allowed to eat in white restaurants in the South. Joe Louis was the toast of the town when he beat Max Schmeling for the World Heavyweight title to dispel the notion of German superiority over the United States, but that didn't change America's perception of black people.

That was the fate of black men during that time. That is the backdrop against which my father's life began—the life he has navigated to this day.

The Stock Market crash of 1929 and the subsequent Depression during the 1930s is the period that was my father's childhood. As sharecroppers, the whole family picked cotton for ten cents per hundred pounds. Pops can remember being in the fields picking cotton before he can recall being in school. His life centered on his extended family and community interaction, the cotton fields, and school. His free time was spent hunting with his mongrel dog Sam. He could sic that dog on an ant, a bug, or a lizard. It didn't matter. Sam would do his bidding. Dad was something of a loner. He had many friends and neighbors, but he tended to spend his free time in the woods by himself. He must have been dwelling on what he viewed as his options in life.

The Laws family owned some land about eleven acres in size. It was suitable for a family home or two and a big garden. Dad's basic outfit was a pair of bib overalls, a shirt, and an undershirt, along with underwear. He wore short underwear during the warm months and long johns during the cold months. A pair of shoes and socks that served for all seasons was also a staple. Everybody wore some sort of cap or hat as protection from the sun. He had a special shirt for Sunday's church activities, and wore it only on Sundays and special occasions. He may or may not have been exaggerating when he said that he used to bathe once a week on Saturday night, so that he would be clean for church. Otherwise, during the week, he washed his face, armpits, groin area, and feet. Of course, he always had a smile on his face while recounting all of this, but I never questioned the veracity of his stories. Visiting the old homestead of his youth, I can easily accept that what he told me was truth.

Visiting my relatives who had remained in the rural community that my father fled, I could envision the harsh but simple life he lived. One of my father's sisters did not get electricity in her home until well after I was in my teens—sometime during the '70s, as I recall. One thing that was always available when I did visit my father's childhood home, however, was an abundance of love and kinship lavished on me by my relatives.

When my father spoke about his own father, it was always with the respect and reverence you would reserve for someone whom you love and admire. My intent in writing this account is for you to hear the same respect and reverence in my tone for the man I most admire in this world.

My grandpa Otis was a hard-working, God-fearing, respected member of his community. He worked hard during the week, rested on Saturday, and along with my grandmother, herded his children to church on Sunday. The community church, Progressive Baptist Church, was just up the road from where the Laws family lived, so there was no excuse for not being in church on Sunday. Even when grandfather worked hard on Saturday, he still made it to his customary spot in the first pew at church on Sunday.

Dad talked about the times Grandpa Otis gave him whippings for youthful indiscretions. Grandfather did not put up with much childish foolishness, and he expected his sons to assume their responsibilities as men at the appropriate time. Prior to that, they were to live their lives under the guidelines he had set. Any deviation from those guidelines was frowned upon. That trait of fatherhood was certainly passed down from my grandfather to my father.

Pops worked hard during his childhood. For that matter, his entire family worked hard. His stories of those days detail how grandfather got up well before sunrise and, along with his children, did the chores expected around the house. After breakfast—a meal that my grandmother prepared for her family every day of her life—Grandpa Otis and all of his children who were of age and physically capable would get on the wagon and arrive at the cotton fields by full sunrise. Their days consisted of chopping or picking cotton, whichever the season dictated. Dad says he had a cotton sack scaled down to fit his small stature when he was five years old. Given his age, there wasn't too much expectation put on him to pick any great amount of cotton, but his training was certainly taking place. His Poppa was preparing him to be able to do a hard day's work, and his being out in the cotton field at such an early age was part of that process.

Dad could make all of us children laugh with his tales of how poor his family was. He told us that his lunch, whether it was during school or in the cotton fields, was always biscuits and syrup left over from that morning's breakfast. His mother put biscuits in an old lunch pail and saturated them with syrup that would be absorbed by the biscuits by lunchtime. He always claimed that those biscuits and syrup tasted as good as anything he has ever eaten. Once in a great while, his mother might put a piece of salt jowl, ham, or sausage in his lunch pail with those biscuits. He was in heaven on those days.

My old man is a tough, durable, and strong man. His childhood helped him become as tough as a man could be. He worked hard alongside his father and siblings, walked just about everywhere he went, and occasionally lived out in the woods, finding food and water for himself. He learned to survive off the land and read danger signs. He learned to hunt, first with a stick or rock and, eventually, with a weapon. He could fish in a river and feed himself. These skills would serve him well in his life.

A good student, he attended the neighborhood school, Canaan Elementary School, an all-black school for grades one through eight. He spent ninth through twelfth grade attending E. A. Kemp High School in Bryan. Kemp High was the high school in town for colored children. He passed all of his classes during school. He was never eager to be called upon by the teacher, but he always responded with the right answer.

He and my mother went to school together from elementary to high school, although he was a year ahead of her. He was athletic; he was good at running track and liked playing baseball as well. He got the hell knocked out of him during his one attempt at playing football, and that was the end of his interest with that sport!

My father's size was not a big hindrance to him. At seventeen, he was a fierce warrior while standing only 5' 7 1/2" tall and weighing about 135 pounds. He commented that as a young boy and teenager, he had his fair share of scrapes with other boys in the community, and he held his own.

My mother recalls that as a teenager my father fancied himself a lover of the ladies. She explains that many times, on the bus to and from school, my father—her future boyfriend and husband—would be in the back seat of the bus with some fast girl from the community, kissing and petting as if there were no other children around. During that time, she viewed my father as a class clown and cut-up. She mentions that he was a handsome black boy with a charm that could sway all of the young girls. While she found him attractive, he was much too loud and mannish for her taste. It wasn't until he was a junior and she was a sophomore in high school that they start courting.

The Old Man often claims that he would have lost his mind if he had been forced by fate to remain on the farm. He despised the work, longed for something more fulfilling, and felt limited by the opportunities that farming in his hometown community offered him.

One day when he was fourteen, he decided he was fed up with working in the fields alongside his father and siblings. He had had enough of the harsh life of chopping and picking cotton. He decided to run away and hitch a ride up north to see if the situation of earning a living was more appealing in the community of some of his relatives. He wasn't looking for easier work but work that was more fulfilling. He left home and hitched a ride some seventy-five miles north to Marlin, Texas.

He had cousins there, and he was able to stay with them and find work. But what he also found was that life was no different for him there than at home. He still had to work in the fields all of those long hours, and the pay wasn't much different. He found that no one showed nearly the degree of concern for his welfare that he had been given back home. All things considered, he decided home wasn't quite as bad as he had thought. Soon after that, he opted to return home to the loving warmth of his mother's embrace and his father's hearth.

Between the ages of fifteen and nineteen, as Dad grew to young adulthood, the respite for him and all of his peers was going to town on Saturday night. Granted, the times were different and the activities were limited to doing things only with other black folk. However, there were plenty of juke joints and hangouts to select from if an individual was looking for something to do on a Saturday night. There were several options from which to choose a gathering place.

My father and his friends would all agree to meet at a specific place and time. Since the main mode of transportation for black men in those days was by foot, my father thought nothing of walking the eleven miles into Bryan. Every once in a while, he could walk up to the highway and hitch a ride into town, as long as it was daytime when he was hitching. Sometimes, a generous person would allow him to ride the running board of their vehicle. Most often, a black person extended that generosity. Seldom, but every so often, he received a ride from a white person.

It was always easier to get a ride into town than to get a ride back out to his house. It wasn't often that a stranger would pick up a black man in town, let alone drive him all the way out to where he lived. It was usually late and some people feared black men—especially after dark! That's how it was in those days.

There were places to dance, sing, socialize, gamble, and drink. A good dice game could always be found, as could a card game or a good fight. Women and men from his and other communities were always circling around each other, looking for that spark. The after-hours black entrepreneurs were certainly out in force at that time of night. Hustling, scamming, pimping, and prostitution, as well as drug dealing were part of the landscape after dark back then. None of these activities appealed to Pops, but they were as much a part of the landscape as work, church, and home. My father recalls a whole host of characters whose paths he crossed during those nights. As he grew to young adulthood, my dad still held the notion that there was something better out there in the world for him. He was yet to realize it, but on December 7, 1941, his life and the lives of all Americans would change forever.

After the Japanese attack on Pearl Harbor, my father's girlfriend (my mother) saw her uncles join various branches of the military. My father's older brother Bert enlisted in the service as well. My father longed to join his brother in the military, but at sixteen he was too young. Within a year's time, many more young black men from the community were joining the armed forces.

By the spring of 1942, my father had finished high school and dreamed of joining the army. He was then seventeen and, by law, still too young to join. He remedied that problem with a bold-faced lie. He gave his birth year as 1924 instead of 1925 and was allowed to enlist into the army. Dad chose the army as a means of escaping the harsh life of farming the land. He left Bryan as a young black man from the outskirts of a small farming town and returned an American fighting man. He cut a dashing figure in his Class 'A' uniform, and as he was courting my mother throughout this time, she says that he was a beautiful man in his military uniform.

My parents had become a serious couple during Mom's sophomore year in high school, and they were madly in love. They both suffered from intense loneliness when they were apart, and their courtship was typical of the times. He would call on her at her grandparents' home, and they would walk down to the river and have picnics under the pecan trees. My mother's people were well off in the community as her grandfather had worked to acquire his land, and they owned well over one hundred acres. My father's people were comparatively lower on the economic scale during that time. There was no fuss made of that difference, though. All of the people living in "The Bottom" knew everyone else, so their courtship was only odd because my mother was rather prim and my father was somewhat roughhewn. She has commented on thousands of occasions that his smile was enchanting, and she always blushed when he looked at her.

One of my favorite stories about my parents' courtship that always makes me smile is the story of the time my father thought he saw "the headless man." It is a story about love, and it is also a story about the thoughtfulness and sensibility of my father. There was a tale that circulated in the community about a headless man that had supposedly been spotted out in the pasture near my mother's home. Over time, it had grown to silly proportions. In fact, several people had sworn that they had seen it.

One Saturday evening, my father went to visit my mother at her grandparents' house. Again, back in those days, walking was the most dependable mode of transportation for a young black man, so that is what my father did. He reached my mother's home, and they had their visit. Their date ended, and by this time it had grown late. With the exception of natural moonlight, the night was considerably dark. (I have traveled the distance between my parents' respective childhood homes, and I will be the first to admit that it wasn't just around the corner. Realistically, it was about three miles.) This didn't bother my father as he often spent nights in the woods with his dog, Sam.

Walking home in the dark was not a reason for any trepidation, and in the interest of time and distance, he decided to cut across some of the open pasture. He began his abbreviated route through a corn-field and out of the corner of his eye, noticed some movement. He stood stock-still and looked and listened in the direction the movement appeared. As the movement of the clouds uncovered the moon, enough light became available for him to make out the silhouette of what appeared to be a stoop-shouldered man with NO HEAD! The silhouette moved and the movement was rather peculiar for a man, if indeed it were a man. A man did not walk in such a stiff-legged manner. As more clouds moved across the moon, the shadows began to cause more confusion. Pops thought that maybe he, indeed, was looking at a headless man. Fear gripped him and he began to sweat. *Should he turn around and start running back to his girlfriend's house or face the headless figure that stood between him and his short route home?* My father was not prone to making rash decisions or doing many things on impulse—a personality trait that rang true in this instance. He stood and studied the headless figure for a moment. Finally, he decided that in order to come to a workable conclusion as to what it was that stood ahead of him in the cornfield, he would have to view it from another angle.

He began walking perpendicular to the route blocked by the headless figure ahead. He walked in that direction for about fifty yards and then took a path parallel to the headless figure. He eventually drew even with the figure and stood still, studying it for movement. As fate would have it, the clouds moved past the moon, allowing moonlight to suffuse the area. The smile on my father's face must have shown his amusement and relief. A mule, intent on taking advantage of his free time in the cornfield, was up ahead. It was contentedly grazing on the abundant delicacy not readily available in its stall. I know that love made Pops visit my mother, willing to face any obstacle in his path. I know intellect and sensibility made him choose to be rational and think through the process of solving the story of the headless man.

My parents were married on August 10, 1944, in Houston, Texas. The story of their marriage is as charming as any fairytale. My folks left town to get married. Yes, they eloped! They caught the bus from Bryan to Houston, and endured the four-hour bus ride to seal their nuptials. Upon arriving in Houston and the courthouse where they had to register to get married, they found that because of their age, they would need one of their parents as a witness for the ceremony. They both realized that the likelihood of that happening was minimal, and so they enlisted the services of a passerby.

My father paid an older black gentleman fifty cents to stand in as his father. There were no questions asked at the courthouse, and the man went merrily on his way after my parents were hitched. Several months later, in December, my father was shipped to England and the Allied European campaign engaging Hitler's army. My mother, expecting their first child, stayed in Bryan with our extended family.

SECTION TWO

---◉---

AN AMERICAN FAMILY ABROAD

My father was in Europe, serving in World War II from December 1944 until October 1945. During his time in the war, he saw much of England, France, and Germany. In March 1945, he was involved in an accident and he was badly burned on one side of his face; an immersion heater exploded when an inappropriate type of fuel was used to light it. The flame from the exploding heater ignited the fuel can, and Dad was in the path of the makeshift flame-thrower. The army sent him to a hospital in Paris, France, where his wounds healed, and he was reunited with his unit, serving his country. With this exception, Dad was spared any more serious injury during that war.

My father says that the weather was the most formidable enemy during his time in Europe. Born and raised in the southern region of the United States, my father was not accustomed to the harsh winter in Europe. He recalls the misery of trying to stay warm during the war. The war in Europe ended in May 1945, but his unit was tasked with destroying all of the captured German weapons and ammunition, so he remained in Europe well after the fighting was over.

My father often commented about the difference in the way a black man was treated in the United States at that time, compared to the way black men were treated in Europe. He said that most of the English, French, and German people saw nothing wrong with encountering and associating with black soldiers. He could not understand how the American descendants of these same European people could develop such an intense dislike for him and his race.

While he was enthusiastic about returning home, he did not look forward to the hateful treatment he knew society had in store for him. Upon his return to Bryan, his wife, parents, and extended family welcomed him home. His namesake, William Arthur, Jr, the first of his ten children, was waiting there to meet him.

My father had served his time in the army and on November 13, 1945, he was honorably discharged. He, along with his young wife and his son, moved to Denver, Colorado, arriving on New Year's Day, 1946. He was a civilian again, working as a custodian and attending the University of Denver on the GI Bill. Life was harsh for a young black man and his small family during that time. Expecting better treatment after having served in the war, my father was bitterly disappointed in the way society treated a black man.

Even his status as a war veteran wasn't enough to overcome the bigotry and hatred visited on black people during that time. The South had become less and less safe for black men with Jim Crow laws, racial prejudice, and unchecked violence against them. My father felt safer in Colorado, but neither he nor his family fared well at earning a living and living a comfortable life.

My father attended the University of Denver for two semesters. Fed up with the difficulty of living the civilian life and with the negative treatment black people received from society, he reenlisted in the army on April 5, 1947, two months after the birth of his second child (my oldest sister, Patricia Yvonne). He was immediately stationed in Japan and lived there with my mother and siblings through December 1949. That month, on the sixteenth, my sister Pamela Yvette was born.

The Korean conflict broke out and my father left his young family in Japan as he was being shipped to the front. My father was in Field Artillery at the time. He was the crew leader firing the 105 Howitzer cannon. As it came to pass, his leadership skills would have to serve him well during his tour of duty during the Korean conflict.

America was at war again, and my father was a sergeant in the army. Harry S. Truman, the nation's president, declared that America could not support a black army and a white army. He passed into law an order that the military become one united entity. That was the beginning of enormous change in my father's life. Black soldiers and white soldiers were fighting from the same foxhole; the circumstances changed many people's attitudes about race relations. A common enemy was creating an uncommon bond between men of the various ethnicities that served in the armed forces.

My father said it was a major struggle at times, but eventually, men of different races and different walks of life began opening up to one another, and the army became more cohesive. In one interview, my dad details some of the positive and negative outcomes regarding that integration. It is a microcosm of what has become of our nation.

Dad came within an inch of being killed while fighting in Korea. A convoy of his artillery battery was en route to a new firing position when his crew's truck had a flat tire while pulling his 105 Howitzer cannon. The crew had to stop at a truck depot overnight and get the tire changed. They had to wait overnight because the truck depot did not have a spare tire at the time.

The next day, his crew was driving along a road and the North Koreans ambushed them. My dad was the senior noncommissioned officer, and he was in charge of the crew of nine black American soldiers and four South Koreans. During the attack, his driver jumped from the truck and ran and took cover in a ditch. The crew was still under fire as my father ordered everyone to assume defensive positions to try and determine the direction the enemy fire was coming from. The firing ceased, so my father ordered everyone to get back on the truck.

He ordered the driver to come out from the ditch and commence driving. The soldier refused! Understanding combat stress, my father directed another soldier to drive the truck and, again, the soldier refused. Pops decided that he would drive the truck himself and got behind the steering wheel.

The truck was on an incline and pulling a Howitzer cannon so he was having a difficult time getting it up the hill. At about that time the truck stalled and his crew came under fire, again. A bullet smashed directly through the windshield on the driver's side of the truck and fortunately, because my father was being watched over by the Supreme Force of Good, it struck the steering wheel right in front of his face. An inch higher or lower and my father would have been a casualty of war and I would not be here.

In that ambush, my father lost three American soldiers and two Koreans, but he was not even scratched. He did experience a loss of hearing during that time of his career, being around artillery fire. He said he'd accept the loss of hearing anytime, compared to being killed!

My father fought in Korea from July 1950 through June 1951. He returned to his family in Japan, and they returned stateside via a passenger ship to Seattle, Washington. From there, they took a train to Bryan, Texas, to see their relatives and friends. In late 1951, my expectant mother and all the children were situated and living in Bryan while my father was stationed at Fort Sill, Oklahoma. Two weeks before the birth of my sister Carol, my father took my mother to Fort Sill to give birth at the military hospital there.

On February 24, 1952, they celebrated the birth of their third daughter, Carol Lynn. My mother returned with her fourth child to Bryan, waiting until my father could find quarters in which they could live. After he secured housing, the family lived in Fort Sill, Oklahoma, until January 1953. My father changed from Field Artillery to the Infantry, and he changed duty stations to Fort Hood, Texas. My mother and the children lived in Bryan, always in close contact with dad's parents. From just after his time in the war in Korea in 1951 until late in 1953, the Laws clan was living stateside, treated like second-class citizens in a society made safe by the sacrifices of black men such as my father.

My mother always admitted that she liked living overseas better than the United States. She did not enjoy biting her tongue against speaking out about the way black men were treated in their own country.

I wanted to know how my mother felt about the historical treatment of black men and black people in general. Taken from a taped interview, these are my mother's comments about living in Japan and Europe and the plight of black folks:

> *Living overseas, my children and I were exposed to a totally different world. Right after World War II, we lived in Japan and I had all of the best of everything. I had a housekeeper and your father had a manservant. We were living on the Japanese economy and we were treated quite well. It was an exciting time because I was a country girl and this was like living in a Hollywood movie.*
>
> *I could go where I wanted and I was treated respectfully by the Japanese. They did not look at me with disdain. In fact, they seemed to prefer blacks to whites in a lot of cases. My children were exposed to a different culture and it was a wonderful learning experience.*
>
> *The same can be said for Germany, whenever we lived there. It was as if being in the American military carried an elite status. Most of our children spoke two languages. My older children spoke three languages! Of course, whenever we returned back to the States, we were relegated back to second-class citizenship.*

About black men and the plight of black people, she said:

> *Society should take the time to think about all of the injustices heaped on the black man and ask: What do you suppose black men's mentality and mind-set should be after over three hundred years of slavery? Over three hundred years of being snatched up, chained, and taken away from all that was safe, familiar, and good in your world. If they could answer that question, maybe then they might get an inkling of understanding as to what has occurred in the psyche of the black man.*

My grandfather used to recount stories told to him by his father about black men getting beaten for standing up straight. Supposedly, the slave master or overseer didn't like to have to look up to a black man. Now I ask you, what kind of cold heart must that require? Pa Dix, my grandfather whose home I was raised in, said that the will of a black man was the first thing that slave masters tried to beat into submission.

A male slave's only worth was his ability to work. If he had a child, it was taken away from him. If he called himself getting married, his bride would be taken from his bed to go and lay with the master or overseer, in his bed. Often, he had to watch his wife bear the child of the white plantation owner. He didn't have any voice in the decisions that were made regarding his family.

My grandfather said that, eventually, a black male slave chose to isolate himself in his real feelings and assume an aloof posture regarding taking a bride and making a family. Now then, if the mind-set of black men, for generation after generation after generation, was to keep his real feelings hidden and disregard his natural instinct to take a wife, have children, and provide for and protect them, how far back must black men travel to reach their center? How far from the dark side must they come before they can even start to feel good about going the other direction and doing what they, in another life, had learned to do?

No one wants to dwell on what black men have had to endure since the beginning of this country. Psychologists and counselors will tell you that an individual's psyche can be damaged in the short time that is his childhood. Well, think of the message beaten into the psyche of black men for all of those years, and you shouldn't have to wonder what psychological bent they might possess. Every single black man alive and all of his male forefathers should receive a medal and some money for the fact that this country was built on their backs.

I would challenge any man alive today to endure the beating administered to a black male slave. Just once, I'd like to hear a white man tell the world how that feels. Now, imagine that beating happening to a man's body over and over again. There could be no healing known that could pacify that trauma! He didn't just have to endure his beatings, either. Imagine having to stand around and watch my father or brother, your uncle, or granddaddy get beat like that and ask yourself what kind of mind-set one would possess after experiencing or witnessing that happening.

My grandfather said that his father told him of men going mad trying to deal with the hardship and doom of being a slave in this country. I can get angry talking about some of the things my grandfather told me about white people in those days. It's as if white people didn't think we had a soul or heart.

The irony is that they would sleep with the black women and impregnate them and the process of birth was exactly the same as it was for their white women. Then, in most instances, the slave owner would treat his own offspring like a slave. Well, hell, anyone with that much evil in their heart, I just don't know what to say about them.

Some people feign ignorance as to what kind of damage all those years of pain and suffering can inflict on a person. What do they expect? Sometimes I think that they knew what they were doing, the lasting damage and all. Feigning ignorance is their way of not having to deal with a heart that would be too heavy to bear, should they accept the responsibility for what they did.

You know, the playing field has never been level. Society is afraid to level it because they know that if black men are given the same opportunity as everyone else, they will probably surpass them in whatever it is they're doing. I think society fears a black man most because after all of the pain and misery it has inflicted on him, to paraphrase Maya Angelou, "still he rises."

The black nuclear family has never risen to the success of our white counterparts. In some instances, and I thank God every day for the strength and perseverance of my husband, a black man who has been capable of providing a comfortable, safe life for his family. But as a group, black men have been allowed less, given less, and assisted less than any other group in the existence of this entire world.

From the time that slavery was abolished, there has been the expectation that being a family man is something that has been easy for black men. It was not easy and became even less so with his lack of opportunity. With no training and minimal skills except those acquired working the land of his owner, many black men were at the mercy of benevolent whites for any assistance they received. That assistance was usually scarce.

There were a percentage of black men whose will was extra strong and they were usually the more adventuresome lot. My grandfather moved from Alabama to Texas back in the late 1800s, and because he was smart, he was able to buy land, a few acres at a time, until he had enough to lease out to white farmers or allow black sharecroppers to work.

Your father's grandfather migrated to Texas from Tennessee, and he did pretty much the same thing. Our families have done pretty well, and for that I am truly thankful. But I tell you, some of the horror stories I've heard about slavery used to make me so angry that I could just cry, or go shoot somebody.

Nowadays, since slavery is unlawful and society can't hold us down that way, the media perpetuates the belief that black men are worthless and useless, citing a few isolated examples of stupid, irresponsible behavior and letting those instances be a blanket indictment against all black men. You know that's not true, though. Hell, your father has been the only example you've ever needed of what a brave black man is capable of accomplishing.

Christine Yvonne Nelms Laws
December 2003

After living in Japan and loving it, my mother was not enjoying life as a military wife stateside. The negative treatment by society in the United States had both of my parents wishing to go abroad again.

On September 20, 1953, while the family was living in Bryan, close to all of their extended family, my sister Cathy Marie was born. In October 1954, my father was stationed in Germany, and he shipped out, leaving my mother and the children in Bryan. He eventually sent for them, and they soon joined him overseas.

Our family lived in Germany from the winter of 1954 until the late spring of 1956. While in Germany, my mother presented my father with another daughter, his fifth. Deborah Louise was born on September 29, 1955, in Stuttgart, Germany. By late summer 1956, the Laws family was back in Texas living at Fort Hood, where Wanda Paulette was born on September 29. It had been exactly one year to the day after the birth of her older sister Deborah.

Sergeant First Class William A. Laws now had seven children; one son—his eldest and his namesake—and six beautiful girls. In early 1958, my dad and our family were stationed back in Germany. On September 1, 1958, I was born in Augsburg.

My mother swears that at some twenty months of age, I could understand spoken English and German and could even speak words in both languages. I do not recall this ability, but I do know that on an aptitude test in linguistics that I took while serving in the army, I scored high enough to have the military's Counter-Intelligence Liaison offer me an opportunity to study languages at their school in Monterey, California. (That's another story.)

We lived in Germany for more than three years and my sister Astrid Diana was born in Augsburg as well. Her birthday is July 26, 1960. We moved back to the United States in 1961, settling back in Lawton, Oklahoma, at Fort Sill. My parents purchased a home at 1760 S. 14 Place. My brother Christie Denique was born there on January 9, 1962. My father had sired ten children in just under seventeen years. God bless and protect the woman who is my mother.

I have known for most of my life the details of my father's childhood and the path he has taken to get where he is today. What I didn't know is what kind of impact particular historical events might have played in his thinking. I asked him to speak on racism in the military and what it was like being a soldier at that time. I asked him about the civil rights movement. I asked him about Vietnam. I asked him about teaching at two different, all-black high schools in Dallas. I have always known about his values and what is important to him. I asked him if, at this point in his life, he had any regrets about his path in life. These are his words:

> When I joined the service in 1942, the military was segregated. There were two armies—one black and one white, except, of course, in the officer corps. The officer corps was all white. They had white commanders commanding the white enlisted troops, and they had white commanders commanding the black enlisted troops. That was a bit of a problem because, as in anything, you have some good and some bad.
>
> Well, there were some good white officers; that is, they had good leadership qualities. And there were some bad white officers. They did not have such good leadership qualities. But you always had to do what they ordered you to do. As far as places to hang out after duty hours, it was still segregated for the enlisted men. Social activities were always separate.
>
> We had to find places that would accept black soldiers. If they did, we were usually all who would be at that establishment, that night. Whenever both groups ended up in establishments that accepted both groups, if both were there, it usually ended in a fight. You know, a brawl of some sort. Of course, that was frowned upon and soldiers often paid the consequences for that. But, like I was saying, there were some good officers and there were a few white enlisted men who had an understanding. They understood our plight. But there was only so much they could do.

If they made too much of a scene, they could and would be called "Nigger Lover" and that sort of thing. They were ostracized and shunned. The same could be said for a black soldier who seemed to want to hang around with the white guys. He was labeled an "Uncle Tom." It was sort of harsh, but that's the way it was.

I know that I joined the army because I couldn't afford to go to college. Momma and Poppa couldn't afford to pay for me. So I joined to get away from the harsh life of farming. I wanted a better way of life than my daddy had.

Now, the army changed in 1948. Harry S. Truman's administration was against segregation in the army. The NAACP was bringing to everyone's attention the mistreatment of black soldiers in the army. Franklin Roosevelt had died in 1945. He didn't necessarily agree with the army being segregated, and Truman sort of took up the mantle and said we could not maintain two separate armies.

He determined that America would have one army, and he signed an executive order that did away with all-black or all-white units. Naturally, that didn't happen right away. It was about the middle of 1950, during the Korean War, that the army began shipping replacement soldiers to the frontline units, and they sent black soldiers to white units. The funny thing was that whenever they did, the white units would claim there had been some clerical mistake and send the black soldier back to where he came from.

The units on the front lines finally started realizing that they were short of strength, and they couldn't keep sending these black soldiers back. They needed the bodies to reinforce the strength of their positions. So it came to pass that it was an accepted thing, integrated units. It really began to be a permanent thing during 1951.

The really sad part about the whole thing was this: After the war, some black enlisted soldiers had earned rank in their old units—good rank like "Master Sergeant." Those soldiers always seemed to come under intense scrutiny from the white officers of their new unit and inevitably, they would be accused of some trumped-up offense and they would lose their rank.

It was a terrible thing—really sad and so unfair because I had several buddies that had earned their rank. They had paid their dues and served well under their commanders and that was how they were rewarded. And because they were men, they didn't take it sitting down. It only worsened the situation. Some of them were busted all the way down to private.

They just couldn't endure the injustice and they physically fought white people because of it. That just made the situation a total loss for them. Some went to jail. Some turned to alcohol and drugs. It ruined men's lives. I was so very fortunate not to have had that happen to me. But it happened to some, and that's a shame.

In my opinion, in the army, things were still better for a black man than in civilian life. It was the 1950s, and I had heard of the civil rights movement but I was at war in Korea and all I can remember focusing on was the dockworkers' strike in San Francisco. This is when I was introduced to unions.

I heard that it was because of the unions that we weren't getting our supplies shipped to us. Now, I'm at war, needing to be resupplied. We need ammunition, rations, cold weather clothing, and such, and the workers are striking. The union is striking. It upset me to no end that they could be thinking about a raise in wages when they had soldiers fighting a war, depending on them to ship us the supplies we needed to survive. That left a bad taste in my mouth.

I know unions are needed to protect workers. I know business will take advantage of workers if the unions don't carry the weight that they carry, but I just always felt that they could have put aside that issue, for that moment, and shipped us what we needed to win the war.

In the late '50s and early '60s, there was talk of war again. I had never heard of the countries of North and South Vietnam and wondered what the hell their problem could be. That is about the time the civil rights movement really began to grow. Early on, I followed the civil rights movement through the media. It wasn't getting the amount of news coverage that it would eventually get, but I remember hearing and reading about it. Of course, there was a political slant on it that caused me to have mixed feelings about it. This was especially due to the fact that I was in the army.

It seemed to me that it started as an issue that focused on the rights of black people and I was in line with that. Then that focus morphed into a political platform for all of humanity. Suddenly, the fight in Vietnam was about our infringing on the civil rights of the North Vietnamese; the fight was about infringing on the rights of the average American. The fight was about things that I couldn't quite identify.

I remember when I was in Vietnam. I was over in that jungle, fighting, and all I heard was Martin Luther King, Jr., and the civil rights movement was marching in protest of the war in Vietnam. Students and civilians were marching in protest to the war. All of these groups were marching against the war. I didn't understand the strategy behind that, and I recall that I was pretty upset.

I felt that the protests were targeting me, directly, and I was at odds with the movement, then. At that time, I thought Dr. King's actions were impeding the progress of the military's war effort. But what his movement was about was bigger than just the war in Vietnam. It was about equality. It was about leveling the playing field in all aspects of life. It was about humanity.

It wasn't until after looking at the whole of what Dr. King's intent was and taking an active interest in finding out more about Dr. King that I understood the movement and began to closely follow his message. The more I heard him speak, the easier it was for me to change the way I had felt from when I was in Vietnam.

In 1969, I retired from the military. It was a bittersweet occasion. I was forty-four years old, and it was sweet because I was freed from taking orders from anyone. I was my own man and I could come and go as I pleased. I was not defined by rank any longer, so in my mind and heart, I was truly equal to any other man. The bitter feelings I have about it are that a lot of good men did their duty and gave the ultimate sacrifice, and a lot of people quickly forgot about those good men.

In the army, you had to respect the rank of an individual regardless of whether or not the individual warranted your respect. Some people of higher rank than me would never have gotten my respect for their person.

It was not as safe for me and my family in the civilian world. Living on the army base, you could leave your doors unlocked and you trusted your neighbors. Your children were supervised and safe if and when you were away. It wasn't so dangerous. In civilian life, you had to watch your back at all times. You couldn't trust anyone. And while it was nice to be out of the army, the civilian community was a harsh cultural shock for my children.

It was very tough on them. They were accustomed to structure and rules. There was a regular formatted regimen. My children were abused in civilian life and I really believe that. My children had grown accustomed to a community that was safe. They had been taught to trust and respect adults. They were taught to be friendly and nonjudgmental. They were accustomed to living life and not being afraid. That is what was very appealing about the military, the longer I stayed in.

My children had the best there was to have. They were exposed to all cultures and folkways. They had seen distant parts of the world. Their minds were very global early in their lives. Civilian life shrunk their world and, to an extent, their minds. I had to be so conscious of their safety that I had to limit their boundaries. Unfortunately, Dallas at that time was a city that was behind the times, in the minds of my children.

I didn't worry too much about my sons. I knew that I would always have a handle on them. I would not lose them to the streets. It was my four youngest daughters that I worried about. I could not control them. They were young women.

Living on an army base, there were activities in which girls could be involved. The girls had as many structured activities as the boys had. Clubs, teams, and associations—there was something for them to be involved in. There was an introduction to coed activities at an appropriate age and it was done under supervision. The army base was a self-contained world, and they always had safe social outlets and activities to nurture children's growth.

I taught my daughters the best I could and gave them all the guidance I could give. But, again, they were women and women attract men. Not all men are honorable, and my daughters actually struggled, living in Dallas.

I don't think any of my children who arrived in Dallas with me back in '69 could anticipate what they would have to experience. I never anticipated it. People were predatory at a very early age. Young black children, girls and boys, were not all innocent and untainted. Some were hard-hearted and hateful. Some had been victimized, and some victimized others.

My children had not ever witnessed or experienced such behavior from children before. My children were totally shocked to hear children use profanity. They hadn't heard too much of it, even from adults. To hear children cursing out one another, their teachers, and other adults used to make Anthony physically nauseated. I felt like this environment that we were living in would profoundly affect my children and it has. It has affected their children as well.

When I was teaching at Roosevelt and Lincoln High Schools, I had to be more than a teacher for some of my students. I had just finished three years as an ROTC instructor at Pratt Institute, and the students there were studying to become officers in the military. They were young adults. But when I came here to Dallas, I saw a group of youngsters, from seniors in high school that were as old as nineteen to kids as young as thirteen years of age.

I saw a group of young people that I thought I could help grow into young adulthood. I saw a group of children, some of whom were interested in knowing what the military was like, what the Vietnam War was all about, and how to be a soldier. I also had some kids who couldn't care less about what the war was about and what being in the military was like. I decided right then that the most important thing I could teach them was how to be good citizens.

By good citizens I meant, teach them to be honest, hard-working, law-abiding, tax-paying participants in this society. I shall never forget one of my students, in particular. He was a young man, about fourteen or fifteen years old. I was teaching the class about how the army works and how the chain of command has to be adhered to.

We had pictures of all of the members of the military chain of command from the President all the way down to our student Battalion Commander, along the walls of our classroom. This youngster raised his hand and asked me a question. He said that if the chain of command was so important and the army would provide such a good opportunity for him, a young black man, how come there weren't any black faces in the leadership positions along the wall and why should he believe in the leadership?

I thought about that question for a while and then I pointed out to him that there were, indeed, black members in that chain of command, and he was right in insisting that they be present along the wall, in the chain of command. I personally wrote a letter to the Department of the Army and asked them to address this issue.

I explained what had occurred with my student and mentioned to them that if I was going to be an advocate of the military and be expected to teach and support the idea that the military can provide an opportunity to young black kids, they should have something to which they could aspire. That inquiry started a national campaign to add to the pictured chain of command sent out to all of the nationally affiliated JROTC schools, the photos of all of the black generals that belonged in the national chain of command.

I received a letter of recognition from the Department of the Army for that inquiry. That young man made me think about the message I was trying to impart to those children. They needed a role model, and I decided that I would be a role model for them.

Some of my fondest memories of being with those kids were when we rode the bus to football games. When we served as the color guard and presented the colors, we rode the bus along with the drill team, pep squad, and cheerleaders. We didn't ever have a good football team, as I recall, but we used to have a good time singing and chanting on the bus. Those kids could surely clown on a Friday night.

That bus would be rocking back and forth and those kids would just be singing and clapping. "We surely didn't win it but we surely didn't give it away." That was the chant they would always end up singing. I will always remember that.

Occasionally, I will run into one of my students in the grocery store, at the gas station, or at the barbershop, and he or she speaks to me and treats me with respect, so I guess I did a good job by them. I always wanted them to know that they could come and seek my advice for whatever problem they had. I still get phone calls from some that have kept in close contact with me.

I have one in particular who went to the military right after graduation from high school. He's about ready to retire now. He is the subject of one of the most amazing stories I could ever recount. When he was in high school, he was my student Battalion Commander. It was his senior year, and he really had earned his rank. He had been in JROTC for four years. He had a good mind for the military, and he was a strong believer in discipline. He made a fine soldier.

Anyway, this particular time, some of his subordinate students had played a trick on him and had locked him out of the school armory. He got thoroughly upset, and he was cursing and swearing up a storm. It just so happened that the principal's wife was across the school courtyard and heard him using all of that profanity.

She reported back to her husband that she had heard foul language being used back by the ROTC armory room. Her husband, the principal, prided himself on being a strict disciplinarian. He went storming back there to see who it was that was using such bad language. None of the students would divulge who the culprit was, and the principal decided that it was my responsibility to get to the bottom of the issue and report back to him.

I knew almost immediately who it had been. I went back to the principal to let him know that I would handle the situation. He was adamant in wanting to dole out the punishment himself but I thought it fitting that I should. Besides, my student commander was a good kid, and I did not see the need for anything too serious happening to him. I asked the principal what he thought should become of the child. The principal wanted to expel him from school. I didn't think that expulsion was warranted, so I didn't let the principal know who the culprit had been.

The incident went without much more notice and was eventually forgotten. Years later, I was sitting up late one night and my phone rang. I answered it. A male voice that I thought I recognized was on the other end. He asked me if I recognized to whom I was speaking and after a moment or two, I realized that it was my former student commander on the other end of the phone.

He told me I would never guess where he was calling me from, and, sure enough, I had no earthly idea. As it turns out, he had joined the military. He was a sergeant in the 82nd Airborne Division and he was part of the force we sent to Panama to capture Manuel Noriega. He was calling me from the captured offices of the deposed Panamanian leader.

I asked him if he could get in trouble for doing such a thing, and he said that it wasn't likely as he was the senior NCO on the site. I asked why he had called me, and he said that since he was in the office of someone so important, he decided to call someone that was important to him. He chose me! That meant a lot to me.

While I was teaching, I wanted to at least impart the same lessons my mother used to always impress upon me as a youngster. She told me to keep myself clean, keep my clothing and surroundings clean, keep my thoughts clean, and stay out of bad company. I wanted to at least teach my students those lessons. I felt that if they would do those things, they would always be prepared to fulfill whatever role their lives led them to fulfill.

As far as regrets are concerned, I don't regret what I've done with my life. I served with honor in the military, and I've taught school successfully for twenty-two years. I have raised ten children to adulthood. I've always provided for my wife. I have lived with as much dignity and honor as I possibly can.

One thing that I will always regret, though, is the fact that I cashed out of a mutual fund back in 1963, and I wish that I hadn't. In 1957, in Germany, I bought into a mutual fund with Dreyfus. I was paying thirty dollars a month into that fund, and your mother and I would only mess with that money in emergencies.

Well, in 1962, I was in Berlin, Germany, and the family was already back in Oklahoma. Christie had been born earlier that year, and around Christmastime we didn't have any money for toys and such. I decided to close out that mutual fund so that your mother and I could buy Christmas presents for the kids. I often wonder how much money I would have now, if I hadn't cashed out that mutual fund.

William Arthur Laws, Sr.
December 2003

My father's words support everything I have ever felt about him. He is the ideal example of a strong black man who has handled his business well and has been a positive role model for his family and his community. He is my hero!

SECTION THREE

---•---

SON OF A SOLDIER MAN

The First Sergeant is eighty-four years old. He's about 5' 7 1/2" tall. I imagine he weighs around 155-160 pounds now, but I remember when he looked and sounded like a giant to me. He could call my name and I would shake—sometimes it would be in fear, but most of the time it was because his call to me meant excitement. The times when it was in fear were because I could be mischievous, growing up. I did a lot of wild stuff. It was risky to my well-being, my health, my safety, and that sort of thing. It was the kind of stuff that a boy can get into when he's growing up and finding out about life and peer pressure and rules. The old man dealt with me, though. You can believe that.

But the times that he called me and I could hear in his tone that he was about to teach me something, I became excited. You see, my dad really took the time to prepare me for life, and his lessons excited me. His lessons have been invaluable!

My name is Anthony, but my dad has called me "Old Buddy" from as far back as I can remember. In my mind it has been as ideal as a relationship between a man and his son could be. I imagine the stars aligned perfectly to allow me to live life as my father's son. My father is connected to my soul, and he is the primary influence in my life. The things I've seen him do, how I've seen him conduct himself, the decisions he's made; all of this has impressed me. I am often totally amazed by the character and integrity that he shows. He does not and will not jeopardize his honor, faith, or moral convictions. I know of few men like my father.

The story of my dad and me is for the most part a fun, funny, happy, exhilarating experience. The few times it hasn't been were definitely because of something I did or didn't do, both as a child and as an adult. It has never been him. While my father is not perfect, he's always been straight, shot straight, and been totally honest and crystal clear in his expectations for me to do the right thing. Thankfully, he has always forgiven me, and we still maintain a fantastic love and honor for one another, and I appreciate that.

My father was a first sergeant in the army until I was eleven years old. A first sergeant is in charge of a whole company of soldiers. His foremost responsibility is the welfare and safety of all of the enlisted men in his company, and that is his primary task. Taking care of soldiers is what he did, and I know that he did that really well because it carried over into everything else he has ever done. He was and is a leader of men.

He's retired now, but he still leads. He is always available to listen to anyone in need of a listening ear. He is always available to help with advice or a few coins, as the case might warrant.

In his spare time, he plays bingo and socializes with all the regulars at the various bingo halls that he and my mother frequent. He just takes it easy now. Hell, he's eighty-four years old and he's entitled. Everything good that he has received, he's earned. With the hard work and sacrifice he has put into life, he deserves all of the good things that come to him.

I wish he didn't suffer so much from the physical ailments that all of those years in the army left in him. I wish he hadn't suffered a stroke in 1994. I wish the arthritis in his back and neck would dissipate so that he could move his neck more freely. I wish his back didn't hurt him so much. I wish he hadn't suffered a physical setback in 1998 that had caused him to spend more time in the VA hospital. I wish his right leg hadn't been so adversely affected because of the stroke, and that he could walk without a cane. Still, he's a trouper! He's a hard-charging soldier, and none of his ailments slow him down too much.

My father was definitely the man of our house. My mom certainly relied on him to fill that role, and he did it. As youngsters, all of us kids revered him then and we respect him now. He's just a good man. He possesses something unique, and I know that it has been a blessing for me to be his son and for him to be my father because he's guided me in just about every situation I've ever found myself in. I want the world to know how much he means to me. He's my foundation.

I think my father's uniqueness originates in the love he had for his father. As I grew older, whenever we would visit Bryan to see my grandparents, it amazed me that my dad, who in my eyes was big and strong and powerful and had total control, would make himself subservient to his father. I remember how I used to be amazed that my dad's voice would soften around my grandfather. His demeanor changed. He would let his guard down a little bit because he was home and my grandfather was in charge. I've always admired their relationship. I admired the way they interacted with each other and the respect my father showed his father.

My grandfather was my role model as well. I know he directly affected the kind of man my father had become. I imagine my father felt the same way about his dad that I feel about my father. Unfortunately, my personal relationship with my grandpa didn't last as long as I wish it had; he died in 1973 before my fifteenth birthday. But his legacy lives on through my father, and Grandpa is still a prominent figure in my mind and in my life.

Along with my father, my mother largely impacted my world. She is one of the Supreme Force's angels, here on earth. She and my father sat on the throne at the head of the kingdom I called home, and she made my childhood wonderful. My siblings and I all have had moments in our adult lives that we probably wish we could have done differently, but we're all here today, alive and healthy and hanging in there in the year 2009 because our parents made our childhood one of love, laughter, and learning.

So it has been and continues to be a great story. I want to leave a legacy for generations to come after me. I want everyone to know how powerful and positive an influence my father has been in my life and the debt I owe him—debt that I'll never be able to repay because of all the things he's done for me.

My father and I have something that I know many black men don't have with their fathers or with their sons. Too many black children are raised in single-parent families and don't know one or the other of their parents. It usually turns out that the father doesn't have a whole lot of influence in their lives, and that saddens me. It makes me wish that they could have had what I had and what I have now in my relationship with my father.

I can remember when I was thirteen years old and it dawned on me that I was unique in my situation of having a father who was always there for me. I played Little League football in 1971, a time when our neighborhood had eleven families with sons that fell within the age range of nine to fourteen years old. We had nineteen or twenty black boys between the ages of nine and fourteen who tried out for, or played for, various Little League football teams in the area.

Of those eleven families, four had fathers who lived at home. Of those four fathers, one was an invalid relegated to a wheelchair. One was a traveling salesman who was often away from home. One was self-employed and took on any odd job he could find to make ends meet, and he was seldom home. Then there was Pops. These four men accounted for only nine of the boys in our neighborhood. The rest of the guys didn't have a father that was at home, or anywhere else, for that matter.

Many black men whom I grew up and went to school with, and worked and served in the military with, weren't fortunate enough to have a strong, positive relationship with their fathers. Some did not have a relationship with their fathers at all. I think it retards a black man's development not to have the proper example, the positive influence of a black man, managing his responsibilities and family shown to him as he is growing and maturing.

We all need a positive example of how to be a man, how to conduct ourselves, and how to be responsible for, and loving to, our children. We all need a positive example of how to love, honor, and respect our wives. I wonder if the black community as a whole has suffered because so many black men don't know how and weren't taught to be responsible men. I wonder if many black men missed the opportunity to experience sitting in their father's lap or at their father's feet while he talked and told stories and spoke wisdom.

Yeah, the Sergeant's eighty-four years old now and suffers from arthritis. He has fused vertebrae in his neck and can't look up without turning his whole body to accommodate his injury. He still has war wounds and carries shrapnel in his body from Vietnam. He has short, curly black and gray hair, a little black and gray mustache and a beautiful smile filled with white teeth. He has slightly stooped shoulders, but he still has a firm handshake. He doesn't run anymore; he just walks now.

He used to run like the wind and was quite athletic when I was growing up. He didn't play basketball well, but he did all right on the backyard hoop that we had. He was good at baseball, and we used to play catch quite often when I was young. He loves football, but after his experience in high school getting tackled, he decided that football wasn't for him.

Track was actually his sport of choice because he could run. I mean he could really run. He could sprint and he was fast, amazingly fast. I couldn't outrun my dad until I was in high school because he could flat out run. In high school, I ran a 4.45 in the forty-yard dash, and he could beat me. He was forty-eight years old at the time! He said that his speed came from hunting rabbits with his dog Sam during his youth. Using a stick or rock to hunt for rabbits, he had to get pretty close to make a kill. Chasing a rabbit is a definitely a way to increase your speed. Old Man had a big grin on his face when he told me that!

The passage of time and the wear of age are both of our realities, but my first recollection of him was, of course, when I was young and quite naturally, he appeared gigantic. I was sort of small as a kid. Well, actually, I was small for my age until I had a growth spurt just before I turned sixteen. But to me, back then, he was a giant!

My father and I have had a fantastic relationship. I love him more than thoughts and words or deeds could ever express. I seek his advice about everything before I seek it from anyone else. I find guidance and strength in his words. He's a shining example of manhood to me. I am proud to be his son, and I want the world to know that.

I think that the backdrop to my early childhood was the most exciting time in the history of the United States. The turbulent '60s and the free-love '70s are the times that were my childhood. I was aware of the rumblings of change that were clearly on the horizon and vividly recall the assassinations of John F. Kennedy, Martin Luther King, Jr., Malcolm X, and Robert Kennedy.

I remember the civil rights movement and images of black people being beaten, sprayed with fire hoses, and attacked by dogs. Before he was assassinated, it seems as if Martin Luther King, Jr., was on the news every night. My father made all of us sit down on the floor and listen to each speech by Dr. King that aired on television.

I remember H. Rap Brown, Stokeley Carmichael, and Angela Davis speaking at rallies and protests. I remember Ralph David Abernathy and the Southern Christian Leadership Conference. I remember the riots at the '68 Democratic Convention in Chicago. I remember when Watts, in Los Angeles, was a war zone. I remember asking myself, *Where is all this taking place?* Because I never saw it on the military post.

I remember the Beatles on the Ed Sullivan Show. I remember when Motown was the best sounding music my ears could wish to hear. I think my big brother had every album that Stevie Wonder, Smokey Robinson and the Miracles, Marvin Gaye, the Temptations, the Supremes, the Four Tops, and the Isley Brothers had recorded at that time. I remember the space program, and rockets blasting off to the moon.

Laugh-In and *The Mod Squad*, as well as *Julia* and *I Spy*, were always on at our house. *Big Valley* and *Bonanza, Batman* and *Green Hornet*—those were all shows that I watched growing up. Vietnam was an integral part of my life because of the fact that my dad had been there, and he was so interested in the news. *The Huntley-Brinkley Report* and the *CBS Evening News with Walter Cronkite* were news shows we watched, every weekday, for a very long time.

"Black Power" and the Black Panthers were slogans and movements and groups that my father felt were necessary but somewhat extreme. Hippie communes and the psychedelic drug scene made a mockery of the establishment and seemed to be the biggest problems of white society. I grew up during this time in America's history, and the times were as important a part of my life as my father's guidance.

My dad was in the military and I think a lot of my personality, a lot of my characteristics, behaviors, ideals, and opinions were formed from the military life I grew up with. In the military, all our friendships and our acquaintances were based on the rank of our fathers or mothers. Not that I remember too many female soldiers in the military then, though. I saw a few, but I don't remember anyone I knew whose mother was in the military. It was always their dad.

Anyway, my foundation was established while my dad was in the military. It could be that my outlook, in most instances, was because I was young and impressionable, and army life had a direct impact on my perception of my father. I have nine siblings who may have seen our upbringing from a totally different point of view than mine. So while there may be differing perceptions of my father, this one is mine.

I don't know how the physiological occurrence of memory clicks in, so I won't try to be too technical in my explanation of my first recollection of my father. I just remember that suddenly he was there. And he made all the difference in the world with regard to the vibes in our household.

When my mother was at home with the kids and my dad wasn't home there was always a high level of noise at any given point in time, with all of us talking at the same time. It could get pretty loud. However, when dad was home the house was relatively quiet. He didn't go for a whole lot of noise when he was relaxing at home.

As I said earlier, my dad is my role model. He's been my role model since I can remember him. We had just returned to the States from Germany, and my first memory of my father was when I was three and a half. It's as if one day, he just magically appeared. I know that it's because I was young that I don't remember him before this.

My early memory of him is of a giant man who would pick me up, bite my neck, and rub his scruffy five o'clock shadow against my cheeks and make me squirm and squeal in laughter. I remember asking myself, *Who is this person, and why is he hugging my mother? What's going on here? Why is he hugging Mom, and why is she smiling like she likes it?* She had a huge smile on her face, that's for sure. From then on, I noticed that she always had a smile on her face, especially when this big black person was around.

He always made her smile. In that instant, he had made a lasting imprint in my memory. From that day on, my memories of my father—his presence and his absence, his anger and his kindness; his love for, and leadership of his family and his desire for what is good, right, and fair—are what have guided me.

I have a few predominant memories of my dad at Fort Sill. I remember we had a German shepherd named Pywackit, and he was killed when an army jeep and then an army truck hit him. Pywackit died, and Dad supervised the funeral we had for him in the backyard of our house.

I remember when I stepped on a nail and had to get a tetanus shot. I remember that it hurt like hell. My dad used to mock me when I cried, and he did so at the hospital when I got my shot. Eventually, I was laughing and crying at the same time. My mother looked over at my dad and just smiled.

When I was young, my dad also frightened me. It was a healthy fear because it was the fright you have as a child when everything and everyone is bigger than you are. It's that self-preservation that is borne in all of us. My early fear of my father was because of his loud, heavy voice. It was a booming, intimidating voice that could not be duplicated by anyone. His voice had this command—I'm pretty certain that it was developed over his career in the military. It was perfected due to constantly having to holler out commands as first sergeants do. I know this because I served in the military myself, later on. (That's another story.) There is some speculation here, but I'm pretty certain that's where it comes from.

Anyway, he could modulate his voice and as he called my name, I could determine by the tone of it whether it was a good or bad call. I can laugh about it now, but I remember that it was terrifying to hear him call my name in the voice that was clearly an indication that I was in trouble.

My father was a firm believer in not sparing the rod, but I have to give him credit for moderation. He was never abusive and didn't go overboard, but he would inflict corporal punishment at a moment's notice. My siblings and I were always fearful of that. I know I was, anyway. Also, being sort of mischievous and sort of wild and loose sometimes, I definitely experienced his belief in corporal punishment.

The Sergeant's voice was a fear-inspiring voice that stopped you dead in your tracks and made you pee on yourself if it was your name he was calling. You were being called to stand and face the music, and that was never fun. Never!

My dad could discipline me with his words and make me feel an inch high, but he also possessed a voice that spoke of safety and care and it cancelled all fear! Sometimes, he'd scold me and make me wish I could disappear, but he could console me and I knew that everything was going to be okay. If he said it was going to be okay, it was going to be okay! His voice caused unmitigated glee if it called my name and I heard love and pride in it. That tone meant I had done something that warranted his special attention and congratulations. He rewarded me with his words and made me feel ten feet tall. It was really something to grow up in his house!

And it was his house—everybody marched to his beat. My brothers, sisters, and I were all allowed to express ourselves and say what we felt and thought, but the final decision was his.

When the Sergeant was away at war, maneuvers, bivouac or wherever he was with regard to the military, my mom stood in for him. Her word carried the same weight. I often try to convey to anyone who will listen to me brag about my parents, the unity between my mother and my father. I can speak tirelessly of their roles in my development.

My mother is a beautiful, loving, caring, kind, compassionate Earth Mother and black woman. She was put on this earth to have ten children and raise them and make sure they were complements to society and not burdens. Because of my father's success, tribute must be paid to her because she is the person who has always been at his side, cheering, goading, cajoling, and inspiring him to be the remarkable man that he is. She did that job really, really well.

My dad has been a lot of things to a lot of people throughout his life and still plays a role in many people's lives. It's just a marvel— the wisdom he possesses, the experiences he's had, the trials and tribulations he endured, and the mountains he's scaled. He has seen it all and knows something worth knowing about.

He is a black man whose contributions, in my opinion, are on par with those of any other black man that we recall historically. It's simply that his life hasn't necessarily been made public the way other prominent black historical figures have been. But if you were to reflect on what my father has done with regard to the people he's had an effect on, you would probably agree that he's almost historical in his existence, or at least he should be.

My relationship with my dad is founded on honesty and trust. He practiced it and expected it. I think that is why he whipped me so much. Looking back on it, I don't think my indiscretions as a youngster were what caused the punishments I got so much as my attempts to lie my way out of what I had done. It's not that I claimed total innocence of the matter but more that I tried to give the idea that I didn't play a very big role in it. However, that was usually a lie because, as a child, whenever I did something I was usually the ringleader or instigator.

That was my nature at that time. I would try to lie to my father whenever I thought that implicating myself would certainly earn me my father's wrath. That is the folly of youth, especially at an early age. I thought I could spin a tale so fantastic that my father would believe it. I thought that the wilder the story, the better. I spun some pretty big tales when my father would ask me what happened. Without ever even dignifying my wild story by questioning me, he would just say, "Go to your room, boy, I'm whipping your ass!"

It did not dawn on me that he usually already knew the details of, and my role in, the incident. His asking to hear my story was his way of determining if I had learned anything from my previous dealings with him. If he decided that I hadn't, he was determined that I would learn something from my punishment.

My father would lecture me after the whipping and make me feel good that he beat me. And to this day, I feel good that he beat me. He was teaching me that our relationship must start with trust and when you trust someone, you must be honest.

He would cry if any of his children lied to him. Dad told me that he was my father, and it was his business to know what was going on in my life. I must tell him the truth at all times so that he could provide me with good guidance and sound advice. I still don't know why I lied, but I never got away with it. My father did not suffer my childish foolishness as I got older.

We lived in Oklahoma until the summer of 1963 when we moved from Fort Sill, to Fort Riley, Kansas. The years in Kansas were a time in my life when I learned how to socialize with other kids. We lived on the army base and had lots of activities to keep us occupied.

The elementary school and the junior high school were on base, and the high school was in Junction City.

It was a wide, open base with lots of space and unless there was bad weather, I was outside with my little friends all day long. We had a big playground area where all the kids hung out; there were all kinds of social activities occurring, every day. There were forests to explore and big hills to climb. A lot of wildlife was nearby, and it was always exciting to spot a deer, a raccoon, or a bobcat.

The most wonderful appeal about the Midwest is the seasons. You get to experience the beauty of each one, and you are always left with a lasting memory of something you experienced during any one of them. I fell in love with snow and the winter season when we lived in Kansas. It was a wonderful time in my young life.

Military life was tinged with tension; our father could be sent away at a moment's notice, and we always felt that apprehension. My father made splashes in and out of my conscious mind when we lived in Fort Riley, but his impact weaved its way into my soul.

I remember certain days in Fort Riley when I could not escape the boredom of having to be indoors, and my father would spend some of his free time with me. He would not pay attention to anyone or anything but me. He did it a lot of the time when my little brother, Christie, was still young enough that my big sisters watched out for him more than I did. He still needed to be held and changed. I was five years old and could fend for myself around the house. I could talk and go to the bathroom by myself.

During that time I was sort of left on my own. Thankfully, I was not old enough to have to change Christie and do all of that kind of stuff for him. I don't think I would love him near as much as I do now had I been forced to take care of him. At the time, we hadn't started hanging out together. I really thought that his acting like a baby was a ploy. Figure me! That was exactly what he was at that time. He was just over a year old but that label had a negative connotation to me, at five years of age.

My father would often catch me daydreaming or wandering around the house, aimlessly, and ask me what I was doing. I told him that I didn't have anyone to play with. Back then, until Christie got older, I had no indoor playmates. All of my friends and I played outside. My mother wasn't keen on having other folks' children in her house, except on special occasions.

Those dull, dreary, indoor days were the times when my father rescued me. We would sit at the table and make paper airplanes and play Old Maid or Go Fish card games. At my age, I was beginning to get the numbers and letters thing squared away in my head, but I had the pictures down pat.

He gave me his undivided attention and that is the time in my life that I starting falling in love with my dad. Before that, I wasn't quite sure who he was, other than the tickle-neck man, but on those days when it was just my father and me, I started feeling a really strong desire to be near him all the time.

He would let me help him shine his boots and the brass for his uniform. We would go upstairs into his room, and he would take out all of his polish and rags and stuff. He would ask me to fill the top of the Kiwi polish container with cold water from the bathroom sink. That was always an honor because he was saying that he trusted me enough not to spill the water or make a mess in the bathroom.

It's amazing the things that impress a son who is loved by his daddy. We had a quiet time to talk and find out about each other's day. He would ask me what I did that day, and I would ask him what he did. Looking back on it, I don't think my explanations of my day made much sense to him and I know his explanation of his day didn't make much sense to me, but it sure was good being near him.

I have always been connected with my mother. We share the same birth sign and only a day separates our birthdays, but the more I hung around my father, the more I saw his smile and smelled his after-shave, the more I heard his steady, soothing voice, the more I wanted to be around him.

Even then, I knew that he was someone special because everyone in the house underwent a personality change when they where around him. He made my mother swoon, giggle, and sing when he was around. My sisters all clamored for his attention in the evening when he came home. Before and after dinner, they gathered around him, competing for his undivided attention.

He was the center of attention when he was at home, so much so that my big brother even exhaled in his presence. To my young eyes, my big brother's chest always seemed inflated except for when my father was around. And I truly believe that he exhaled out of relief because Daddy was home, and he could be a son and not the man of the house. That was the vibe that my father gave off, and still does, to this day. Whenever we're around him, we are his children.

I think the fondest childhood memory I have of my father (and I have hundreds of fantastic memories of the things he did) is bath time. I was about five of six years old, and Christie was a toddler of two. My dad made it a regular happening that he would give us our bath. That was the greatest thing two little black boys could ask for.

A bond between my father and his sons was forged during that time because we learned to trust him. He would tell us to lay back and put our head in his hand so that he could wash our hair. I remember that it wasn't the easiest thing to do for me. Feeling the water in my ears and along the sides of my face was more than enough to make me want to get up and out of the tub. I remember Dad saying, "Trust me, son." I asked, "But why?" And he said, "Because I'm your daddy and I love you, and I will never hurt you and I will always protect you." I would finally lie back in his hands and let him wash my hair and you know what? No water got in my face and no soap got in my eyes, and I didn't accidentally swallow any water or anything. I loved him!

And he made me love him more. He made me want to please him. I behaved for my mother and didn't cause my sisters too much grief. I looked in awe toward my big brother Bill, and I watched out for and later hung tough with Christie. But I always wanted to make my father proud of me. He inspired me to achieve from a very early age. To see him smile and nod his head in acknowledgement of my achievement was my motivation; his words of praise made me feel lightheaded.

He could make any achievement seem small compared to his praise for it. Being on the 'A' honor roll was not as exciting as hearing him announce to the whole house that I made the 'A' honor roll. His praise was that powerful. All of his children were made to feel that way. He made us feel special in achievements that merited special praise from our daddy.

Now based on what has been said, you would think that those instances of praise were long-winded affairs comparable to a coronation, but in truth his praise was one three-syllable word. It was a word used exclusively as the highest recognition for performance, in my father's house. That word is "Outstanding!"

Whenever my father used that word as praise for something one of his children did, we felt like royalty. And he, my mother, and the rest of the children were obligated to treat the recipient of that praise as such. It was special—my father's house.

SECTION FOUR

—◉—

LAUGHTER AND TEARS

My earliest memory of my father and I having an interaction that really impacted the way I felt about life was the time he taught me about what being afraid means. It is a story about using reason and common sense, and it is a story that provides a microcosm of my life.

I was about six years old. My mother sent me down into our basement for some of her sewing supplies. It was past sunset and into the early night when she sent me, and I was always terrified of the dark. I usually entered the basement during the daylight hours. It had a little window for ventilation, and light always filtered through so that it was never totally dark. Also, the light switch was at the head of the stairs and flipping on the light switch was no great challenge to me.

Well, this particular time my mother sent me down there it was growing dark, and I needed the light on to feel comfortable about being down there. I turned on the light and made my way down into the basement. While I was in the middle of searching for needles, thread, and a thimble for my mother, the basement light bulb suddenly burned out causing the basement to go dark—an immediate and terrifyingly complete darkness in that huge sub-ground-level room.

Suddenly, it was pitch-dark, and I couldn't even see my hand in front of my face. I let out a scream that would have peeled paint! Everyone upstairs came stampeding down the stairs of the basement to see what had happened to cause such a blood-curdling yell. By the time my parents and older siblings had reached me, I was almost hysterical with fear. I must have been down there in the dark, completely alone, and unable to see anything for about, oh, say twenty or twenty-five seconds. Someone must have hit the light switch on the way down to rescue me and realized that the light bulb had burned out because the beam of a flashlight soon cut through the total darkness and shone its light on me, standing mortified in the middle of the basement.

Initially, my parents and siblings were concerned that maybe I had fallen and injured myself because they all answered my call to be rescued. Imagine their reaction when it was determined that I was fine and that my urgent cries for help were merely the result of being marooned in the complete darkness of the basement.

That was the earliest I can recall my father being upset with my reaction to adversity. He looked at me as if I had done something that terribly disappointed him. I, on the other hand, was just happy to be saved. He took that incident as an opportunity to teach me a lesson. He became adamant that I should know the difference between being afraid and being caught in an unexpected situation. In screaming as if I were being assaulted, I unwittingly initiated what I like to refer to as the "enlightening!"

After the rest of the clan, seeing my situation and determining they were not needed, made their way back upstairs, my father and I changed the light bulb in the basement. That is when my lesson began. With the light on, I was instructed to stand in the middle of the basement and look around and identify various items that occupied its space. The hot water heater was noted, as were the washer and dryer. My big brother's bed and his nightstand were duly recognized along with all of the boxes of junk and stuff that a basement always seems to contain.

After I made note of all of the various things in the basement, my father told me to stand right where I was while he went back upstairs. I must thank him now for not closing the door, for his next action in my lesson was to go to the top of the stairs and hit the switch on the wall, casting me into darkness. However, I was still able to see a little bit because the light from the dining room upstairs was visible through the open basement door.

My father called down the stairs, asking me if I was okay. I responded that I was fine. Then, he closed the door.

Well, I wasn't feeling the lesson so soon after my episode, and I began to scream again. Only this time no one came to my rescue. At the time, it seemed to me that I screamed for a long time. Looking back on it now, I would venture to guess that I screamed for about fifteen seconds before my father opened the door and hollered down that I needed to "shut my ass up" because there was nothing wrong with me. I immediately shut up. He hollered to me to just stand where I was and look around. I did as I was told and stood there looking around the dark room. Eventually, after a moment or two, I was able to make out the shapes of the things that I had earlier identified. The washer and dryer were still there. Across the room, I saw my brother's bed and nightstand. Yes, and those were the boxes of junk and stuff I had seen when the light was on. *I think I'm getting your point, Dad!*

After standing alone in the middle of the basement for about five minutes, I was able to see everything I had always seen during the daytime or when the light in the basement was on. Imagine that! I climbed the stairs, opened the basement door, and stepped into the dining room. My father sat at the dinner table with this shit-eating grin on his face and asked me if I had learned anything. Thinking that the lesson was over, I commented that nothing in the basement had changed except that the light was either on or it was off. I also noted that after a time, a person could see almost as well in the dark as he could in the light. My father smiled, and I knew that I had absorbed his lesson well. He patted me on my butt and sent me on my way.

You think the story is over, don't you? Well, think again! I had pretty much forgotten the entire episode in a little more than thirty minutes. That was more than enough time for my father, along with my mother and all of my older siblings in on the plot, to create the next scenario in this tale.

I was upstairs in my bedroom, ready for bed in my underwear, tee shirt and socks, and minding my own business. One of my sisters told me that my mother wanted me. I immediately hopped up and went downstairs to see what my mother needed. She was sitting in the living room sewing hems on dresses she was making for my sisters. She asked me if I felt better about venturing down into the basement and I told her that I did. She said, "Good, I need you to go and get my thread from down there." In the hoopla, I had forgotten to get it. I didn't see any problem with that; I had just now conquered my fear of that dark, dank place and wanted to redeem myself for my earlier behavior, anyway.

Off I went to get the thread. Now, please understand that at six years old, I was easily impressed, easy to forget, and not thinking about anything much of the past or future as I was making my way to the basement. It was the same basement where earlier I had had visions of the bogeyman assaulting me. (We pronounced that monstrous imaginary figure the "boogeyman" as did all Southern kids.)

I left the living room and headed toward the basement. I had to pass through the kitchen and dining room to get to the basement door, and I was keen on trying out my newfound courage. I chose not to turn on the light in either of those rooms, as I made my way to the basement door and that is something that I will reflect back on as being the stupidest move I had yet to make in my young life. My father knew his son, and he played me like a fiddle! The door to the basement opened out into the dining room and as I pulled on the doorknob, there was some resistance. I pulled a bit harder, and still I could not get it to open. Finally, I really gave it a serious tug and it came open in a rush.

All that I can clearly recall is a growl, the head of a monster, and my turning and running! The bogeyman was real and had come up from the basement intent on getting me! A yell that would have the police responding immediately was the loudest noise I could hear and it was coming from my mouth. The growl of the bogeyman was close behind, and I had to escape.

A dark dining room created an obstacle course that I somehow had to navigate in escaping the basement bogeyman. The clean, shiny kitchen floor was like quicksand to me in my slippery socks. Oh, save me, the bogeyman was closing fast and I was at my wits' end! Like

Jim Brown bowling over a hapless tackler, I knocked over a dining room chair. The extended wall that divided the dining room and kitchen made an excellent pivot point for the less than ninety degree turn I was going to have to make to escape the fast-closing bogeyman. My God, he was hot on my heels!

Something reached out and grabbed the back of my underwear. I was not that partial to them. The bogeyman could have them if he wanted; I just needed to be rid of them if I were to escape. That was my demise; too many holes requiring too many different bodily contortions made shedding them only wishful thinking. I was destined to become a victim of the basement demon that had haunted me all of my previous days in this house. *Tell my family that I loved them!*

The bogeyman had me by the waistband of my underwear, it was dark in the dining room and kitchen, and I could not reach the living room and the safety of my parents. Hey, wait a minute! I didn't see my father when I had come downstairs to see what my mother had wanted. Where was he when I needed him most? Where was the man who could do battle with this basement demon? Could he not hear the anguished cry of his pursued child? "Daddy, help me!"

The bogeyman snatched me up by the seat of my underwear! It had me in its arms, and I could not escape. I was doomed, yet I gallantly fought on; I kicked, screamed, and lashed out with my little fists and teeth. I had to make my escape. The bogeyman lifted me off of my feet and tried to carry me away. Aha, it did not know its way around the house! It was carrying me into the living room. The living room, where my mother was and, hopefully, where I would be rescued by my father.

My mother sat where I had left her, a smile of amusement on her face. My older siblings stood, doubled over, all laughing uncontrollably at the spectacle. But I still didn't see my father! I heard a muffled voice behind me that sounded vaguely familiar. Strange, the bogeyman sounded almost exactly like my dad! I turned to the voice and saw my dad in a military chemical mask. My father had donned it as part of his setup to scare me shitless, and he had done an exemplary job. I belatedly realized that I had peed all over myself. I had to laugh at what everyone else was laughing at—me. Laughter and tears have always been a part of my life!

Another incident—one that left a lasting impression in my mind—occurred during that same period. It is not a light, funny tale but one that teaches a life lesson just the same. It is branded into my brain forever.

I had this friend, a little white boy, whose father liked to explore the outdoors and would often take us walking in the hills behind the housing area in Fort Riley. Custer Hill was a famous natural landmark in the area where we lived and it was a wonderful place, with opportunities to climb the hill and explore the old Indian trails and markings there.

This particular time, my friend asked me if I could accompany his father and him on a walk through a wooded area near our house. I ran home and asked my dad if I could go. It was about three o'clock in the afternoon on a beautiful fall day. The air was warm, and the leaves had turned all of those magnificent colors that leaves do in the fall. I had on my new sneakers that got for my birthday. Some comfortable, worn jeans, and a sweatshirt completed the perfect attire for that after-noon, and that's what I was sporting. It was a marvelous day to be a little black boy! To my dismay, Pops told me that it was too late in the day to go off exploring. Dinner would be ready soon, and it would be growing dark and, NO, I couldn't go.

Disappointed, I walked back to my friend's house to tell him that I could not go exploring with them. As I walked, I got the silly six-year-old notion that if my father didn't see me, he could not know whether I went to the woods with my friend or not. What I didn't know is that during the time that I was walking to my friend's house, my father had called my friend's father, and the two of them decided that

I could, indeed, go with them to the woods. My father told the man to let me know that I had permission to accompany them, and I was even going to be allowed to eat dinner at their house because we'd be returning late. Do you see what happens to kids sometimes? I had a good thing and didn't even realize it!

I got to my friend's house, fronting like I had been given permission to go with them. That boy's dad looked at me as if he had seen a premonition. He repeatedly asked me if my father had said that it was all right for me to go with them and I repeatedly answered, "Yes, my father said that I could go." He looked at me with what I now know were the eyes of a man who knew a certain little black boy was going to get a killing when he returned home later that evening. And he wasn't going to save me. Yes, I know that look, now. Nothing else was said about it. We had a fantastic time, roaming through the woods that afternoon and evening!

That man, a fellow soldier of my father, that man who was also raising a son, let this son learn a lesson that day. You see, when we returned to my friend's house later that evening, I was supposed to eat with them, but I did not know this. I was as hungry as a little boy could be but when they offered me dinner, I could not accept it because I was supposed to be home for dinner. At least, in my plan, I was supposed to be home for dinner.

With my father's permission that I could accompany them, my friend's dad was in no great rush to finish our exploration. My friend's dad was going to feed me dinner, and he knew this. I did not know this because I had lied to him about getting permission from my father to accompany them. He, in turn, let me suffer in my lie. I could not have gotten permission to accompany them without that call from my father. My story to my friend's dad about getting permission was a lie. I had lied on my father by saying I could do something that I had been told I could not do and saying that the words were my dad's words. I had to lie when I was asked if I would like something to eat.

I was so damn deep in this lying business. It was about seven o'clock when I finally extricated myself from the presence of my friend and his family. I lived about three blocks away, and I broke out of their house at a dead run. Three blocks' dead run by a six-year-old will lose to a phone call, going away!

I got home, as hungry as all get out! I got home, as tired as all get out! I got home, as afraid as all get out! Funny thing is I didn't even know what I was afraid of. As far as I knew, I had gotten away with this small indiscretion. But when I stepped into the home of my father, everything that had been beautifully seen, heard, and done that day was made cold, ugly, and painful by my lies.

I suffered what was to be the worst two hours of my short life. I encountered my father; my lies had created an angry, disappointed, demonically mean, forlorn, black man. He was angry for all of the lies I told him, each lie spun off of the one before it. I got a whipping for those lies. He beat me for the first lie and all of the lies spun off that lie! He beat me for all of the lies that I would ever tell him! He attempted to beat the act of lying, out of me. He did not permit lying. He did not permit it at all!

And then he spoke to me. He spoke to me, and I heard his disappointment in me, in every word that he said. He spoke to me and his disappointment in my behavior, judgment, and thinking was so utterly apparent that I could not bear to look at him. I could not bear it anymore, so I ran! I ran and hid away from my father like I was diseased and not worthy to be in his presence. I hid because I knew that after his disappointment, I would feel his demonic wrath. The whipping was never the most hurtful aspect of my father's punishment, but his wrath was insufferable. I was about to suffer!

The food that my father had set aside for me was not for me to eat. I was told to go into the kitchen and look at it. I was told that I had to see what I was not going to get, as payment for my lie. I was not allowed to speak, nor was anyone allowed to speak to me. My mother, whose loving arms I longed for, ignored me. My older brother and sisters walked past me as if I did not exist. Christie, who would have spoken to me anyway, because he was young and did not understand, was corralled and kept away from me, as was my little sister, Astrid. I was a ghost in my father's house.

I went upstairs and took a bath and got into my bed, but it was not yet over. I did not know when it was going to happen, but I knew it was on the horizon. The final testament to the damning effect of my lie was yet to be realized. As I slipped into a fitful snooze, I was shaken awake by my sister Carol and told to go downstairs and apologize to my father for all of the wrong deeds that I had done. With each dreaded step, I felt like I was on a trip to see a relative on death row.

My father was downstairs in the living room. There was no light save a small lamp on the end table next to his chair. My mother sat across from him, and the room was empty except for the two of them. The look on her face was so noncommittal as to seem like the face of an expressionless wax figure. My brothers and sisters lined the stairway leading upstairs, and they peered down like owls in the night.

I approached my father and saw that he was crying. It was not just that tears were coming from his eyes, but no, he was weeping. His body heaved repeatedly, and he looked like he was being torn apart from inside out. I did not know what to do or what to say. I did not know what to think, but then again, I did.

I began to think about how hurt he must be to cry the way he was crying. I had cried like that, and it was because I was in pain. I began to realize what pain he must be feeling if my behavior could make him react as if he was physically hurt. I was frightened and dismayed that I could do this to the man I loved so much. My daddy raised his head and looked at me in such sorrow that I would have rather become lost in those beautiful woods than to see that look again.

I reached to touch him, and he cowered away. A feeling so devastatingly sinister coursed through my body such that I became lightheaded and hysterical. He grabbed me by my shoulders and pulled me close to him. He kissed me hard on my mouth and whispered to me, "Please son, don't ever lie on me or to me, again." Laughter and tears, yet again!

My sister Wanda and I laugh about some of the antics and anecdotes of our childhood. There is something unique about our relationship. For whatever reason, she has always willingly been the straight guy to all of my comedic aspirations. She has been the fall guy for a plethora of my stunts and the subject of quite a few of my experiments. She has always been a good sport about my shenanigans, and we always laugh about how big a sucker she could be for my pranks. Wanda played tough but she was really such a tender child. She liked to think that just because she was older, she could do some of the things that I did. I was game to see if she could hang, just as long as she went first. I've saved myself many a disappointing outcome by letting Wanda go first. She didn't ever catch onto that aspect of our interaction until quite sometime later in our lives. Oh, sometime later—like adulthood, maybe! Some of my pranks were really not so funny and again, Wanda, I apologize for the stories I am about to tell.

It was one of those days when outside wasn't hoppin' and being inside was a recipe for catastrophe. Wanda and I found ourselves engaged on one of those occasions, when we didn't heed mom's warning that if we kept elevating our silly behavior, something stupid was bound to occur.

Our mother was a magnificent seamstress. She could turn our house into a clothing manufacturing plant in the blink of an eye. She always used the dining table to cut all of her patterns, making it all but impossible to eat there. Sometimes, when she was really pressed for time, she could be magical!

Once, my mother sewed seven dresses for our seven sisters in two days. I left for school on the day that she was going to the store for material and patterns, and when I returned home, she had cut the patterns and prepped them all for sewing. The next day, I left for school and when I arrived home, seven dresses were on hangers in our dining room.

On this one fateful day, Wanda and I were just sort of hanging around, in and out of our mother's hair, as she worked magic on her Singer sewing machine. We were sitting at the dining room table and my mother had her sewing box right there, easily accessible to both of her restless children.

My mother had a sewing tool that looked like a pair of pliers except that they had pronged pieces between the jaws of them instead of the serrated surface of pliers. The tool was used to attach snaps and catches to material. That was its *intended* use.

But I saw an opportunity to test it as a different sort of tool. I wasn't sure, but quite possibly they could be used as a tool for torture, as well. And I visualized an unsuspecting victim, as I sat there. *Yes, of course, Wanda would make a willing subject. Shall we try? Oh, but of course! What can she say except no?*

"Wanda, put your thumb right here like this." *Yes, yes, my dear!* "How does that feel?" Light pressure was initially applied. *Hmm, no signs of difficulty, thus far. Perhaps, I might apply a bit more squeezing pressure, hey?* "Well, how about this?" More pressure is applied to the handles, just so. "Well, what does this feel like?" And then the devil took over! I closed that snap-mounting tool on Wanda's thumb, and the look on her face was worth the beating. Anyway, I commenced to put four neat little puncture wounds in my sister's thumb.

My mother, who was sitting right there next to us, was so deeply engrossed in her sewing that she did not realize what we were doing until Wanda let out a scream that pierced the calm silence of our house.

I probably wouldn't have gotten a serious whipping had my mother not had to rush Wanda to the hospital for a tetanus shot. My behavior caused a delay in completing her sewing project, and she was livid with me. She didn't make my day when she uttered those infamous, dreaded last words, "I'm telling your father just as soon as he gets home."

From that moment forward, I dreaded the remainder of day. I was thankful, however, for that fact that this whipping would be no more than my just punishment for acting like a moron. The whipping was of little consequence. Of course, it hurt and I cried, but it was not an "event" like some of my whippings had been. The thing I remember most about the entire episode is that my father sort of laughed while he was lecturing me about bringing harm to my sister, Wanda. He said, "Shit! That was pretty damn stupid of that girl to put her finger in there."

The next incident that occurred between Wanda and me that resulted in my getting a whipping from my father was one that was on par with the thumb-puncturing episode. There's something to be said for letting your kids go outside to play. There is way too much dangerous devilment for children to get into indoors.

Wanda and I were again in the dining room of our house while my mother was sewing. This time we were playing a silly game of "can you see me" through the crack in the leaves of our dining room table. I got down on my knees under the table and looked up through the crack in the leaves, to see eye-to-eye with my sister. For whatever reason, we found this really amusing at the time. Of course we always took turns so that next she would be the one on her knees under the table, peering up at me through the crack. We did that exercise twice each when, suddenly, I decided to spice the game up, so to speak.

I waited until Wanda was situated just so, and I asked her, "Can you see me now?" While she was adjusting her position to better meet me, eye-to-eye, I was surreptitiously easing the salt shaker over toward the crack in the table. At just the moment when I knew she would answer in the affirmative, that indeed, she could see me, I shook some salt in her eyes. She came out from under that table as if she were running out of a burning building. She probably thought her eye was on fire. My mother smacked me around the head and shoulders for a few seconds and then went to see about her daughter. Over her shoulder, I heard her call out that yes, indeed, she was going to have my father whip me when he got home from work.

I'll always recall with fondness the way my mother greeted my father when he arrived home in the evenings. They had a ritual that was love, acted out. I didn't see the ritual greeting that day! That day, my daddy wasn't through the door and in the house for five seconds before my mom went off on me and told him to whip my ass. I don't think she even gave him his good evening kiss before she told him that she wanted him to hem me up. My dad looked at me as if to say, "Boy, what have you done, now?" I had this sort of hangdog look about me, while my mother explained to my dad what I had done to my sister. Man, Pops didn't even take off his army uniform before he beat the hell out of me! So much laughter and tears!

On a nondescript day in June of 1965, my father went away. He was a soldier, and his country called him to duty. Looking tall and strong, seemingly undeterred by the tears in the eyes of his children, my father grabbed my mother and hugged her for an extended moment and then boarded a train that would deliver him to the West Coast. From there he would board a ship that would carry him to a little-known country called Vietnam.

His six-year-old son, his eighth child, a child who didn't really comprehend his father's job or the danger that accompanied it, stood silently crying. Tears from a place I had not known flowed freely down my face. I missed my daddy already.

I know a lot of things occurred while my father was away at war, but for the life of me, I do not clearly recall much of it. I started the second grade, and I went to school every day. Before the end of the school year that I was in first grade, and before my father left for Vietnam, I often got into it with my first grade teacher,

Mrs. Howdeshell, because I was a rambunctious child. She and my father spoke often because of my adventuresome manner and hyper behavior.

But during the second grade, after my father left, I was just plodding along, going through the motions. The seasons changed. Summer turned to fall; I turned seven years old on the first of September. I was in love with my second-grade teacher, Miss Retter. All of her students thought that she was the greatest because she could spell her name backwards. Her fiancé was a soldier, and I remember that she anxiously awaited his return, just as I awaited the return of my daddy. During the school Christmas program, she and another female teacher sang a song for the soldiers in the war, and it was such a sad song that I cried uncontrollably during the program. She and I seemed to be suffering from the same malaise and heartache!

I lived through the time but it had little meaning. I did not withdraw, nor did I alienate myself from my family and friends, but I was not the same child. My life was out of balance because my daddy was not home. Often I cried myself to sleep, longing and wishing for his presence. My father was away at war for thirteen months, but the time dragged as if it were an entire lifetime. Every day, the sun shined and day turned to night, but I existed in a fog of despair. My mother tried to console me, and I love her for all of her efforts but I wanted— no, I needed my daddy! Thirteen months passed before the sun shone again for me! So little laughter and so many tears for this little black boy that missed his father!

I was seven years old when my father came home from Vietnam. In my fifty years of living, I can't recall a more profound moment than when I realized that our father was home from the war.

As I played in the front yard of our home, I spotted a figure coming down the street with a duffel bag slung across his shoulder and a kit bag in his hand. My little sister and brother were outside with me, along with a group of my playmates. The gait of this man was familiar to me, but I wasn't completely sure that I was seeing what I thought I saw. Suddenly, a voice rang out and called me. "Old Buddy," it called!

My heart rate increased and a lump the size of an orange welled up in my throat. My entire body first went weak, and then it began to vibrate. In an instant, I heard nothing, felt nothing, and said nothing. I just started running! I ran as fast as I could possibly run, and I don't think my feet even touched the pavement I ran on. Finally, I was close enough to see the smile that was my life. My daddy was home! If you've ever experienced the ache of missing someone you love and then he finally comes back to you, you may know how I felt. The man who was everything to me had come home, and I was overwhelmed with joy!

We moved from Fort Riley, Kansas, to Miller Army Airfield on Staten Island, New York, during the summer of 1966. I had not yet turned eight years old. My memories of my father in New York are forever ingrained in my mind because he became the primary influence in my life. He was always home, and that made him the go-to guy for me.

The best word I can use to describe that time in my life is *Camelot*. I lived in what to me was a perfect world. It was as if I were a prince in some fairy tale who experienced all of these wonderful, exciting childhood adventures. At that time in my life, my father was everything to me. Sometimes he was the evil dictator who prevented me from being free and untethered. Sometimes he was the benevolent ruler of his kingdom, and he would let me run wild. Sometimes he was my master, and I was his apprentice. But, always, he was my father and I was his son.

He taught me how to fix my bike, mow the lawn, take care of my dog, and manage my schedule of chores, homework, and playtime. He was my teacher in Sunday school, and he taught me about having faith in a force more powerful than myself. He was my Den Dad in Webelos, and he taught me all the rules of being good and fair to my faith, my fellow man, and myself.

We played baseball together, ran races against one another, and exercised together. I was never far from his side, except when he was at work and I was at school. I liked being instructed, guided, and encouraged by him. I got more whippings during the years that we lived in New York than at any other time in my life. I guess he felt a need to closely supervise me, too.

My father was very keen on us being educated, and he did not allow any of us to take school lightly. We arrived in New York in midsummer; I was going to turn eight years old on September 1. The few weeks of summer before school started were spent getting our house in order from the move and then getting to know the neighborhood. I was feeling pretty good about all of my new friends on the base, but the school was going to be a public school and not a post school. That meant I was going to be attending school with a lot of people who, in addition to being white, were not going to know how the military operated. I was going to have to watch out for myself, as my father put it.

My first obstacle was getting into the third grade. Public School 41 was the name of the elementary school that the children on Miller Field attended, and in the state of New York a child had to be a specific age for a certain grade by August 31 of that school year. In Kansas, the date was September 1, and that allowed me to be in the correct grade for my age without having to be held back. When my parents went to register my sisters and me, there was some question as to which grade I should be placed.

I remember my father was adamant that I be allowed into the third grade because I had completed the second grade in Kansas. The guidance counselor wanted me to repeat the second grade because she felt that "Kansas schools were not on par with the schools in New York City." My Pops was not hearing any of that nonsense, though. He suggested that there was something that they could do. There must be a test that could be administered to allow me into the third grade, or something. The counselor pounced on the opportunity to make an example of my father being misinformed. She escorted us to the principal's office and explained to him (Mr. Carver, the principal) that my father was being unrealistic in his demand and that there should be no disagreeing with her assessment of my abilities. However, she had not attempted to make an assessment of my abilities. The principal sided with her, but he did provide us an opportunity to make a case for ourselves. He suggested that my father select a book from his bookcase and have me read from it. Bless his heart, he didn't know what he had just stepped in. (A little background music, please.)

I was a little black boy of eight years, and my entire life had been spent in the company and care of six big sisters. I will give you one, maybe two, guesses as to how early you think that I was my sisters' unwilling student in "school." Does anyone know what six girls play when there is nothing to do in the house? Can anyone guess what I was exposed to from the time I could walk and talk? Can anyone imagine the reward to the daughter of the First Sergeant who brought his young son to him and said, *"Daddy, watch this. I taught Toadie how to read."*? Or even, *"Daddy, watch this. Toadie knows all of his numbers."* And I won't even mention the pride I felt in performing all of these "stunts" for him. I was trying to read for my father when I was four or five years old!

My dad chose a random book from the shelves of the principal's bookcase. As is the case in instances when you feel you know that the moment is bigger than you, and your father looks at you with that look that says, *make me proud*, I clicked into my show-off mode.

As I sat in the chair, the book that my father had selected was hanging over my lap until I could not see my feet. I sat up straight, cleared my throat, and merrily began to read about some English settlers who came across the Atlantic Ocean and settled on the northeastern shores that became New York, Connecticut, and Virginia. Mom was sitting in a chair, just sort of leaning back, taking it all in. The principal and the counselor were staring tight-lipped but impressed, and there was Pops with that smile that makes my breath catch in my chest!

I began the third grade in Mrs. Augenstern's class the next day. After my year with her, she recommended that I be put in a class for smart kids. It was great. My father's laughter and that counselor lady's tears!

My dad was active in the community and the church during this time in my life. He and my mother attended every extracurricular activity of all their school-aged children. We were all encouraged to try different activities. I have to admit I am the only one of my father's ten children who didn't learn to play a musical instrument. I didn't worry, though, because for a long time, I have been practicing an instrument of my own—yes indeed, this writing instrument!

My dad encouraged me to join the Cub Scouts when the opportunity came. He thought it would be a good, structured, socially expanding activity for me, and I will forever be grateful for his support. I had a fantastic time in that organization but now, in my opinion, it seems to have lost some appeal. (That's a whole different discussion, though.)

I remember when, as a Cub Scout, I participated in an annual event that is held in the Scouts, called the "Pinewood Derby." All of the scouts purchase a wood carving kit; they are supposed to whittle a car out of a block of pinewood, attach the wheels, and paint the car. The race was held at the next pack meeting when all of the dens met, about a month later.

I remember that my father would not help me carve my car out of that piece of wood. He would watch whenever I took a notion to work on it, but he would never assist me. He said that it was a project meant for me to accomplish on my own. His close proximity was to ensure that I didn't cut my fingers off or something similar.

My car looked really ugly when I was finished with it. He

asked me if I had done the best job I could have, and I said I had. Looking back on it, I don't think I could have done any better than I did, except maybe for the paint job. I didn't paint mine; I colored it with colored chalk. I don't think my dad appreciated the fact that I named my car after a word I'd heard on the news. "Psychedelic" was a buzzword in 1967, and I named my car the "Psychedelic Mobile."

When we got to the pack meeting, and I saw all those other cars, I almost opted not to race mine. Some of those cars looked like they had been created in various automobile research and development departments. I'm talking about sleek and shiny. Some of them had customized plastic windshields and steering wheels. Plastic wasn't even in the kit! Some had the engine carved into them. Some were carved down to dragster style. Mine was just a minimally whittled, horrendously colored block of wood with the wheels attached and ready to race.

Some of my friends' fathers had a huge role in the design of some of those cars. I doubt that any one of those kids used his Cub Scout knife to whittle his car. You could certainly tell that I had. My Den Leader, Michael (Mickey) McChesney, (a full bird Colonel in the U.S. Army now) talked me into taking my car out of the sack I carried it in. Some of my fellow cub scouts laughed at my car, but I would have the last laugh. Ha, ha! I took second in the race! You should have seen my car rolling past some of those pretty cars on the way down that incline. My best friend and one of Mickey's little brothers, Terrence Patrick McChesney, won the event. We had the two ugliest cars of all!

I remember my den had to perform a skit at our monthly Cub Scout pack meeting one time. It was toward the end of the year, and we made up a song that we sang to the tune of *Auld Lang Syne*. I still remember the words to the song that my father helped six ten-year-old boys compose.

May our den never be forgotten
Wherever we may go.
Remember love and kindness forever
Will set our hearts aglow.
We only have one life to live
Let's live it the right way
By doing good in all our work
And just as good in play!

We sang that song in front of the rest of our Boy Scout pack and got a standing ovation. I will never forget that for as long as I live. (I saw Terrence again in 2003 for the first time in thirty-three years, and it was a blessed event.) So much laughter and so many happy tears!

On my birthday in 1968, the Labor Day holiday was also being celebrated, and my father had instructed me to mow the yard. He said that it would probably be the last time we would mow the yard that season. I also had asked for a bicycle for my birthday present.

My dad and mom left the house during the late morning, and I had been told that I should have the yard mowed before they returned. The kids in the neighborhood had planned a big softball game for that day, and I was anxious to get the yard mowed so that I could head down to the ball field. I got the ingenious idea that I would just cut down the dandelions and taller grass around the yard, thereby saving myself some valuable time and speeding up my arrival to the softball game. My nine- going on ten-year-old mind was truly at work.

I wove an indiscriminate path all through our yard, cutting down yellow dandelions and the odd tall patch of grass. Upon reviewing my work, I was satisfied that my father would see no dandelions and tall grass in the yard and feel like I had done an acceptable job of mowing his lawn. How innocent was I? Actually, how stupid is the better question to ask.

Several hours later, my father had arrived back home. I was in the middle of a heated softball contest when one of my sisters arrived at the ball field and informed me that my father wanted to see me at home, pronto.

Having received this directive, I knew not to linger too long after my sister left. I jumped on my pony and high-tailed it to the house, arriving just about the time my sister did. I tried to determine from her face whether or not I was in trouble. She was very quiet, and I felt the ominous threat of doom in the kingdom as I walked into the house.

My father was waiting in his chair for my arrival. He stood up and walked right past me out of the house without saying a word. He walked to the front of our yard and stood on the sidewalk. He quietly asked me to join him. Once I assumed a position beside him, he began to walk to the far corner of our yard. He arrived there and did a perfect about-face and stood, looking back at our yard. He asked me to join him from that viewpoint and to turn around.

I did as he instructed and looked back at the yard. The sun was sliding down the blue sky and the shadows cast the lawn clearly, without the glint of the noon sun. That same noon sun hadn't afforded me the advantage of seeing how stupid my idea had been. My stomach fluttered; then it went sour, and I became nauseated. I was looking at a lawn that had indiscriminate paths, crisscrossing, curving, and irregular, cut into the yard and, save me, it looked really bad. I heard the death knell.

He extended the index finger of his right hand and said, "Get upstairs, I'm whippin' your ass!" I realized immediately what I had not done and that was cut the yard correctly. Just as quickly, I knew what he was about to do and that was whip me. Earlier, I had the notion that I was not going to get away with not mowing the yard correctly, but the big softball game was calling me and . . . and . . . and . . . I had to go, and . . . and . . . you know . . . it was the last cutting of the season. Did it really make a difference in the greater scheme?

According to the First Sergeant, it most definitely did. He lectured me and made me feel like an unappreciative son. He made me wish I had done a good job in the first place. He scolded me, and soon I was nodding my head in agreement, that yes, he needed to whip my ass. So he did!

My father and I had a ritual that we went through when I was to get a whipping. He would always allow me time to try and compose myself and prepare, mentally, and physically, for his whipping. He would wait patiently while I took deep breaths. He would allow me as much time as I needed to finally have the fortitude to put both of my hands at the foot of my bed. He would always whip me in my underwear. He would hit me about ten or eleven times, and I used to see how long I could last before I started crying. In my younger years I'll admit that I couldn't last too long. Maybe about three licks were as far as I got. By the time I was ten or eleven years old, I could hold out until about the fifth or sixth lick. I used to count them, and I don't ever recall him going past twelve. After this particular whipping, I didn't cry too long. I figured that I deserved it.

He told me to stay in my room until I stopped crying, and then I should come downstairs because he had something he wanted me to do. I sat on my bed for about three minutes, regaining my composure. I went to the bathroom, washed my face, and then I went downstairs. Everyone was gathered in the living room of the house, and all eyes were on me as I came down the stairs to ask my father what he wanted me to do. Everyone had a smile on his or her face except me, and I began to get suspicious that something else was going on. My father got up from his chair and went into the dining room. He was there for only a moment, and then he returned. He was wheeling my birthday present into the living room: a new five-speed, banana-seated, high-rise handlebars, purple Stingray bicycle. He had a huge grin on his face, and that made me feel like everything was all right between us. I started crying all over again and really felt bad for not doing a good job on the yard for him. He had come through for me, and I felt like such a cad. But I learned about honesty and integrity that day!

I remember the following spring when I went to my father and asked him for a dollar. He looked at me like I had lost my mind. He said he did not feel like he should just give me money without my earning it. He then suggested that an ideal way for me to earn my own money was to mow the neighbors' yards. He said that while it was early in the season, I should start asking people in the neighborhood if they needed their lawn mowed. He said that even if they turned me down now, maybe later on when their grass had really grown out, I would be the first person they would think of to mow it for them.

Sure enough, his plan worked, and soon my Friday evenings and Saturdays were booked with lawn-mowing jobs. I had one especially good weekend mowing yards, and I had earned nineteen dollars. For a nine-year-old going on ten, nineteen dollars was a pile of money, and I felt like I was wealthy. Dad let me do whatever I wanted with my earnings. I used to buy comic books, baseball cards, and junk food.

One particular Saturday, since I had earned so much money, I asked my father if he would take me to the local five-and-dime store and the doughnut shop. We jumped into the car and off we went. I asked my father if there was a limit to how much money I should spend, and he said that since it was my money and I had earned it, I could spend whatever I wanted. I decided to stash ten dollars so I asked Pops to hold it for me. I figured I could spend the other nine dollars. I purchased a James Bond model car, some comic books, and a dozen Bavarian cream-filled doughnuts. I still had change left over, too.

We arrived home and all of my sisters and my little brother were asking me for some of my doughnuts. I selfishly turned them all away, except Christie. I told him he could have one of my doughnuts because he was a boy. I told my sisters that girls had cooties and didn't deserve doughnuts. They weren't too happy with me. My sisters went whining to my father that I was not sharing my doughnuts and he said that, by rights, I did not have to give them any. I had spent my own money, and I could decide what I did with whatever I bought. My mother suggested that I was going to spoil my appetite, eating all of those doughnuts, but again the First Sergeant told her that I could eat them all up if that was what I wanted to do. You know the lesson is coming, don't you?

I proceeded to eat eleven Bavarian cream-filled doughnuts, and in a short while, I was as sick as I could possibly get. If I told you my stomach was a little upset, that would be comparable to calling Mount St. Helens a little hill. I turned green behind the gills, dizzy in the head, and got rubbery at the knees. My stomach got queasy and started bubbling, and I started to drool. My palms were sweaty, my skin got clammy, and I wanted to curl up into a little ball and die.

I ran upstairs to the bathroom holding my hand over my mouth to stop the anticipated eruption and violently vomited into the commode. My sisters laughed at me, and I felt totally miserable. I was so weak that I actually crawled from the bathroom to my room down the hall. I was too weak to pull myself up into the bed, and none of my sisters would help Christie get me off the floor. They told me it served me right, being so selfish with my doughnuts. My father came into the room and took a look at me. He sort of chuckled and shook his head. With this sarcastic smirk on his face, he turned and walked out of the room. I lay there in misery and told myself that I would never, ever be selfish again. But I did learn about greed and overindulgence that day!

I recall 1968 as being the year that my father started teaching me about the world outside of my secure life on the military base. Until that time, I did not know that hate, bigotry, and evil existed. I thought the worst thing that could possibly happen to me was that I would get into trouble for doing something silly, and my father would have to give me a whipping. I did not realize that black people were not treated equally. I did not know that some fathers did not take care of their children. I did not know that the country that I felt so proud to be a member of was a country that didn't really care if I succeeded or failed. I did not know that the establishment didn't think I was worthy of the same opportunities as everyone else. I had no idea that my ethnic group was being targeted as a people other ethnic groups wanted to exterminate. I did not know that some white people had so much evil in their hearts that they would kill black people just because their skin was dark.

My father was just beginning to tell me some of the stories that would color my views of this world for the rest of my life. His stories frightened me. He demanded that I pay more attention to the news and the progress of the civil rights movement. He urged me to listen to what people were saying, read the newspaper, and stay abreast of current events. He emphasized that what was happening then would have a direct impact on my life and I should know which road to travel down as an adult. He started scaring me a little bit, but I trusted that everything he said was true and it was. To me, 1968 was the last year that I was a carefree, innocent child. It was the last time that I recall not having to think about the dangers of being a black male in this society. Guarded laughter, unforeseen tears!

SECTION FIVE

CULTURE SHOCK

On September 1, 1969, I celebrated my eleventh birthday. This was also the day my dad officially retired from the military and we arrived in Dallas, Texas. It was a totally new world for a kid accustomed to living on a military base—a world that, unbeknownst to me, wasn't as friendly as the world I had grown up in. As a child, I didn't realize what a small world I lived in. I was born and raised up a military dependent. I never liked the term "army brat." We weren't brats, as I recall. In fact, my encounters with children outside of the military identified who the brats were. Anyway, I didn't know people existed with so little discipline and order. That's a shock that still sends shivers down my spine—but that's another story.

The most profound difference between living the military life and living life in the civilian world was the lack of rules and regulations in civilian life. I think that my siblings and I were poorly prepared for what Dallas, Texas, in 1969 had to offer us. Having experienced a world that was so protected and regimented until that time, we had not been exposed to the lack of parameters and limited thinking that was the prevailing attitude of the black community in Dallas at that time.

We felt a cultural shock for a long time after we moved to Dallas. The first shock was the fact that teachers had lower expectations of black children in school. I was in the sixth grade and had been in advanced-placement courses from the time I was in the fourth grade. In New York, I was in an academic program called IGC (Intellectually Gifted Children). I was exposed to languages, the arts, civic responsibility, and advanced learning. I was always encouraged to excel at my studies and compete with the predominantly white student body in the school I attended.

My father always told me to expect no quarter and to give none. I was accustomed to being held to a higher standard than the general school population and expected the same environment when we arrived in Dallas. I was totally shocked and amazed at the lack of effort and expectation in the school system that I became a part of. I later discovered that there was, indeed, a higher expectation for excelling. It was just not to be found in the schools of the black communities.

My father learned of the performance chasm between the white schools and black schools of the city, and I was transferred to a predominantly white school. This didn't occur until the eighth-grade.

To give you some idea of what school was like, visualize this. My sixth-grade teacher, a sweet, young black woman, actually apologized to my parents and me because she did not have anything to teach me. She told my father and me that I was so far ahead of my classmates that she did not have any books or teaching outlines regarding what I should be studying.

A large majority of my sixth-grade year was spent tutoring the slower boys in my class. I spent about 60 percent of each class hour going from classmate to classmate, reviewing their assignments and assisting them in trying to understand what our teacher was trying to teach. I recall being challenged only in the math class and the library during my year in the sixth grade. Mathematics had always been interesting to me, and I had a great teacher named Mr. Baree. He made learning geometry and algebra more than just numbers and formulas. He explained the practical application of math to life and made mastering it a worthwhile undertaking. The library books allowed me to remove any and all boundaries and visit faraway places in my mind. Reading challenged my reality and helped me dream of doing more than what I saw young people in my community doing.

There was little change during my first year of junior high school. I was often ridiculed by my peers for wanting to do my class work or homework assignments. I was regularly harassed and threatened by bigger kids who tried to take my money, clothes, shoes, and anything else that they could bully from me.

I would often arrive home nervous from having to evade and escape some dim-witted juvenile delinquent. It would always be some fourteen-year-old giant, still in the seventh grade when he should have been in the ninth, who had promised to bash my brains in because he didn't like that I was clean, spoke clearly, and had a quarter in my pocket and an ink pen that worked.

My dad explained that those children who had it in for me were jealous of my abilities and envied me my worldliness. Pops and I laughed when I replied, "Hell, if they want to know what I know, I'll teach them how to learn it if they'll stop chasing me long enough."

The only saving grace for me during seventh grade was that I tried out for the seventh-grade football team. I found a love for the game and a respect from my peers because I was not afraid to compete against boys bigger than I was. I met a few guys back then who ended up being friends of mine long after we graduated from school. It was really tough at first, though.

My father became worried about me during the year I was in seventh grade. I had taken to sneaking a steak knife from the kitchen and hiding it in my sock or my book satchel and carrying it to school with me. I had decided that I wasn't going to be intimidated by my peers any longer. I think my dad realized he had to do something before a tragedy occurred because I had made up my mind that if I was going to be victimized, I was going to fight back.

He did not punish me for taking that steak knife to school, he just asked that I not do it anymore and to let him know if anyone tried to harm me in any way. He said that he would handle it. I trusted my father to protect me!

On more than one occasion, my father had to reassure us that it was okay to be afraid of what we were experiencing. I was twelve when a boy I went to class with was shot by some kids from another junior high school just because he was a good basketball player. He recovered but was never able to play basketball the way he did before. My sister, Wanda, saw a fourteen-year-old boy get stabbed in the hallway of her school. Both Debbie and Wanda got jumped and beaten up by a gang of girls while they were in junior high school. And I can't even count the number of fights that my brother Christie had before he was even in junior high school.

I made the A and B honor rolls five of the six grading periods during the seventh year of school, and I did not do even a day of homework. I made that honor roll without ever studying for a test. I had a math teacher who was so mean and abusive that she used to make me feel like I was someone's redheaded stepchild. It wasn't because of the treatment that she directed toward me, but more in the way she spoke to us students. Her language was as salty as that of any teacher I have ever known, male or female. She was known throughout the school for her punishment technique.

She had a leather strap, and she used to hit her students in the open palm of our hands as hard as she could with that strap whenever we misbehaved. It didn't matter if you were a boy or girl; she would hit you with that strap. She never had cause to hit me with it, but I did allow her to do so once. I let her hit me so that I would not be singled out as the only boy in the class who had not felt the sting of her strap over the course of the school year. However, I don't see how anyone would rather receive that punishment than to do his or her work.

I had a history teacher in the seventh grade who gave us a test one time, after advising the class to study the practice test at the end of the chapter he had assigned. That day, I glanced at the practice test at the end of the assigned chapter and determined that I could quickly review it. After reviewing it, I realized that the first ten questions of the practice test were true and the last ten questions of the test were false.

On the day of the test, everyone moaned and groaned about the test that he had told us we would be taking. I was totally aghast at this reaction. How often did one get to take a test from the study test in the back of the tested chapter? Preparing for that test was a no-brainer for me.

At the start of class, everyone was given a final opportunity to review for the test. No one took advantage of that opportunity, and 90 percent of the class failed the test.

It was so unbelievable. My teacher had, word for word, copied the practice test that was at the end of the chapter and with the exception of his reversal of their order, the test was duplicated. I saw that those questions that had been the top ten on the practice test were the bottom ten on the new test and vice versa. It took five minutes to review all of the questions, about five more minutes taking the test, and then I took about five more minutes just so no one would accuse me of trying to make anybody look bad. I was still the first one to turn in the test by about fifteen minutes.

I went and sat at my teacher's desk to discuss the test. He asked me if I thought I did well, and I said yes. He asked me if I noticed anything peculiar about the test and I told him I did. He asked me if I would share my thoughts with him and I said sure. I told him exactly what the case had been, and he said that I was exactly right but that most of the class would fail it. I didn't believe him, but as kids brought their tests up to his desk, he gave me mine to use as a master and told me to grade the tests that he handed me. He selected the tests with the names of individuals he thought would fail. He was correct without even looking at the tests—he knew the students that well. On the other hand, I was shocked!

I do have to thank that man for his kindness and support, though. He is the teacher who suggested I sign up for the honors program, beginning in my eighth-grade year. In my estimation, he was a good teacher and would have made himself into a great one had he not had to endure what we all had to endure during that time. He was my homeroom teacher as well, so we often had time to speak about things personally. He used to tell me that I was wasting my brain power, attending the school I was attending.

By then, I could see that my father was necessarily concerned for our welfare. He was at his wits' end to find a solution to our problems of living in civilian society, and I know that he prayed for our safety every night. To this day, Pops apologizes for my having to endure attending sixth and seventh grades under such adverse conditions. The two years I spent in all-black schools showed my father that I needed a change of venue. Assistance came in the way of a program that allowed me to go to a predominantly white school.

The Dallas Independent School District had been planning changes to the status quo because of a lawsuit brought against the city by several minority groups, accusing the city of not doing anything about federally mandated integration. Apparently, no one thought that the Supreme Court ruling in favor of integration meant that anything had to be done because no changes had taken place. Finally, a decision was made that allowed children, at schools where their ethnicity was the majority school population, to transfer to schools where their ethnicity was in the minority population. It was called the Majority to Minority Transfer.

Once the transfer program was launched, my dad initiated the paperwork for all of us to attend better schools. This decision impacted my life almost immediately because I was going to have an opportunity to attend a predominantly white school. In Dallas, some white people and even some black people may not like to remember how uneven the playing field was for black children during the '70s. Unfortunately, it was uneven, and I lived it firsthand.

The very next year, I found myself attending a predominantly white junior high school, and, as fate would have it, I would have to defend myself there, as well.

It turned out that the white kids at the school I attended hadn't had to deal with black kids who could compete with them in the classroom, either. They were a bit taken aback that a black boy knew what they knew, could speak as well as they spoke, could read as well as they read, could do math as well as they could do math, and even knew some things they didn't know. None of them had ever been overseas. Not many of them had seen the big city of New York. In those days, not too many of them had ever even been outside of Texas.

I was one of two black students at the entire school who was in the honors program. There were about 150 black students at the school. With the exception of physical education, a chunky black kid named Phillip was the only other black kid that I ever went to class with for two years. It turned out that his dad had been in the navy and he was born in Germany, just like me. That was where our similarities ended, though.

Phillip was less athletic and more studious than I was and even though we were in the same classes, our groups of friends were different; I hung out with the jocks and he opted for the chess club members. We both gave each other moral support, though, and we were always cordial to each other.

The major differences in my new school environment were the safety concerns and the teachers. The white teachers taught school, and that's all they ever had to do. Violence and acting out were not permitted and those white people were having none of it. I think that my black teachers had way too many peripheral issues to concern themselves with, unlike the white teachers. I know of several instances when black teachers had to concern themselves with what was going on in the home lives of their students and it took away from their ability to concentrate on teaching.

Sometimes, my black teachers had to be concerned with their own safety, not to mention the safety of their students. I saw instances when the parents of some of my black schoolmates would come to the school and physically confront black teachers. I doubt the white teachers had to contend with that type of thing much.

Because my father was a teacher, he identified with the shortcomings that the black schools suffered as a result of the times.

Once again, he provided me with guidance on how to take advantage of the opportunity to attend the white school. He advised me to conduct myself in a dignified manner similar to Martin Luther King, Jr. He said that I should always look for nonviolent solutions to problems with my new classmates and to turn the other cheek. I adopted a version of that behavior, but I ignored the part about turning the other cheek. I never started a fight, but I did not run from one, either.

One thing that I remember most about that time is how hard my father worked to assist his students. He taught at an all-black high school, and he helped his students in school and in their home lives. He taught his charges about the military, as was the expectation of a JROTC instructor, but he also taught them about basic living and survival skills. He taught them the skills they were going to need to live productive lives in our society.

Sometimes my dad would let me read some of the papers turned in to him by his students, and we were saddened at how inarticulate and nonsensical some of them were. I was in the seventh and eighth grades and would help him grade some of the papers they turned in, and I was often ashamed at how badly written some of those papers were. He would sigh and smile a little, but I could tell that he was upset at how far behind mainstream America some of those children were. He took it as a personal challenge to help as many of them as he could, and he had some grand successes due to his efforts.

During his second year of teaching at Franklin D. Roosevelt High School, one such student touched his heart, and my father did everything he could to see to it that this particular young man experienced success during his high school days. The story is one of tragedy and triumph. During the 1970–71 school year, this student wasn't the smartest kid in class, but he had a very outgoing personality and was a nice young man. Dad used to comment on how well-mannered this kid was.

During the first semester of his senior year, this young man's father died, and his mother had to start working. That left this teen with a lot of unsupervised time. He began hanging out with the wrong crowd, missing assignments, and skipping class. His mother was totally unaware of this; she was working late into the night and got home well after dark. The young man was in danger of failing the last semester of his senior year and was not going to graduate. His mother voiced her hopes to my father that her son would finish high school and have a chance at obtaining a decent job. Toward the end of the school year, the young man came to my father and asked for his help because he was failing school.

My father took it upon himself to personally meet with all of the boy's teachers and determine what could be done so that this student could graduate. A plan was formulated, and the specifics were laid out for the young man. He was diligent in his efforts to do what was asked of him, and my father assisted him each step of the way. He was able to meet the requirements for passing those classes he was failing. He was then able to graduate. My father said that one of the most enjoyable moments he has ever experienced as a teacher was seeing the look on that boy's mother's face when he walked across the stage and received his high school diploma.

In 1983, the final chapter of the story was revealed to me when I ran into a man in the parking lot of the apartments I lived in as a young adult. I thought I recognized this gentleman's face and asked him his name. He verified what I was thinking: This is the guy that Dad helped to graduate from high school, way back when. Sure enough, I told him who I was and he broke out in a warm smile and started to shake my hand and hug me. He asked me how my father was doing, and I let him know that Pops was fine. He said,

"Tell your father this for me. Tell him that without his trust in me, his belief in me—tell him that without his faith in me and respect for how I was

feeling, having lost my father— tell him that without his love, and I know it was love for me—tell him I wouldn't have made it. Tell him that because of him teaching me and showing me how to do things the right way, I made it. Tell him that I'm doing well and I have a wife and a daughter. Tell him that I have a good job and I'm happy. Let him know how much I think about him all the time. Let him know what he means to me, having helped me through that difficult time. Tell him that I'll always love him and never forget him. Tell your old man that for me, please!"

I learned what it meant to have set an example of good moral character and perseverance that day!

My father started teaching at another high school in 1973, Abraham Lincoln High. The school was in the heart of the depressed black neighborhood that is South Dallas. My dad likened it to a war zone, sometimes. He taught at Lincoln for twenty years. He has numerous stories about teaching at Lincoln and, I'll tell you, they would truly amaze you!

About the time all of this was happening with my father and his teaching career, he and I were growing closer and closer. I reflect back on my situation and I think that instead of moving further away from my father, emotionally, which often happens when a child becomes a teenager, I moved closer to him. Without him, I probably would have gotten lost. My environment was not always safe, and peer pressure and youthful enthusiasm stirred my soul. The streets were beckoning me, and I felt torn between doing what some of my friends were doing and what my father expected me to do. Fortunately for me, my dad always made himself available. He and I talked regularly about proceeding cautiously through my teenage years. Thankfully, he was totally open and allowed me to be totally open with him.

I had friends who became fathers at thirteen and fourteen years of age, and my father pointed out to me how many lives were affected when something like that happened. He provided clarity to the picture that was my teenage experience.

Because the girl I liked lived just across the street from us, my dad kept an especially keen eye on me and forbade my being across the street when he wasn't home. He was a strong deterrent to my getting caught in any compromising situations. Rarely was he not home when I was, and rarer still was the time that I was across that street. He gave me strict instructions that I was never to be over there if he was not at home and my girlfriend's mother was not there. I didn't understand until later, how he was influencing me. I opted for sports rather than girls during that time.

I was into football in a serious fashion at thirteen. Dad and I always had something to talk about because I was pretty good and he was an honest critic. I can count on one hand the times my father missed one of my games from the time I was thirteen until I was in college. His presence became such a ritual that I could not perform well if he were not in the stands. I did not try to impress my coaches or teammates with my ability. I only tried to impress my father. My father wasn't really conscious of how important sports were in the black community.

Initially, he was amazed at the fervor with which communities supported their high school and Little League football teams. Eventually, it became a crucial part of our lives. Pops cautioned Christie and me that sports were not the only thing we should aspire to be good at. He made it clear to us that we had to be well-rounded individuals.

My little brother and I were among the best players in the city when we played Pop Warner, junior high, and high school football. We were quite popular in the neighborhood, at school, and in the community at large. Everyone knew our names and always had nice things to say about us. My father taught us to be humble and gracious in receiving the praise, so we were. Of course, in our room behind closed doors, we strutted around like we were gladiators. We never showed the public how cocky and confident we were in our abilities. We dared not show that cockiness in our father's house—not in his presence, at least. But behind closed doors, we used to tell each other how BAD we were.

My father used to prepare a special breakfast for Christie and me when we played Pop Warner football and had a game on Saturday. He would take us for a leisurely run in the park around eight o'clock in the morning, and then we would go to the store of one of his teaching buddies, and he would always buy ham steaks and a dozen eggs, some honey, and a loaf of bread. When we got home he would cook those slabs of ham, those eggs, make that toast and honey, and we would drink apple or orange juice. That was serious grub, and it was our ritual back then.

I played running back and I wore number thirty-three. That was the same number as Duane Thomas of the Dallas Cowboys. He was a local role model and had attended Lincoln High School, where my father was now teaching. He was the antithesis of the football role model that everyone expected him to be. He shunned the press and made inappropriate comments about his teammates and the Cowboys' coaching staff. He even spoke negatively about the general manager of the Cowboys, Tex Schramm. He was my role model! He was a black man unafraid to stand up for what he felt were the injustices heaped upon black America and black men. He spoke his mind, and he could tote that mail! I patterned myself after him.

I remember one game I played in when I was thirteen. The team I played on, the Oak Cliff Cougars, was racially diverse. We had about five or six black boys, about eleven or twelve white boys and about seven or eight Hispanic boys. We were hosses, too! My coach in Pop Warner football was a famous high school kicker in Dallas. His team won a big game back in the day, and he kicked the winning field goal. His name is Buzz Terry. He was a great influence in my athletic life.

This particular game, we were playing an all-white team from Mesquite. We were playing on their home field. It was about one in the afternoon. It was a typical fall day in Dallas, warm and breezy without a cloud in the sky. It was about seventy degrees and perfect for football.

I touched the ball ten times that game. I scored six times in those ten touches. After that, Coach Terry took me out and let the other guys run the ball. I didn't play the second half of the game. I took off my shoulder pads and helmet, stuffed my game jersey into my helmet and put all of that stuff in my dad's car. I went back to the field after halftime wearing my favorite jersey, this worn-out, practice jersey from South Oak Cliff High School. It was a number 31 jersey like Donnie "Quickdraw" McGraw's. He was one of the star running backs for South Oak Cliff High School a year earlier.

I was standing on the sideline of my game watching my teammates crush the Mesquite team and a middle-aged black man walked over and stood next to me. He asked me if I knew who was playing. I told him, yes, the Cougars and the Longhorns.

He said, "The Cougars—ain't that the team with that kid, Laws, runnin' for them?"

I said, "Who?"

He said, "Laws, Anthony Laws—you know, that runnin' back they got."

I said that it was.

"Did he get hurt or something? I don't see him out there."

I said, "They took him out of the game already. He scored six touchdowns in the first half, and the coach doesn't think he needs to play anymore."

The man said, "Well hell! I'll just be damned. The only reason I came out here was to see that boy run. That boy sure can run! You ever see that boy run with the ball, son?"

I told him that I had.

He said, "Ummph, I sure would like to meet that boy. He plays football like you supposed to play it. You know, his daddy teaches over there at Lincoln High School."

I smiled. He stood by a while longer and then he decided to leave. He extended his hand and said, "Well, young fella, it's been good talking to ya. Take care, and maybe I'll get to see that Laws fella play next week."

I shook his hand and as I bid him farewell, I told him I certainly hoped he got to see Laws play next week, as well.

When I told my dad that story he asked me why I never introduced myself to the gentleman. I said, "I just liked hearing him say our name. I don't like people knowing it's me they're talking to, sometimes. It's more of a compliment when they don't know it's me. Then it's more like they're spreading good news, not trying to impress you. He was just so animated and serious. He was paying so much respect to our name that I just wanted to keep listening to him talk."

I came in contact with a lot of people in that manner. I loved that people were talking to me about me, and they didn't realize that it was me to whom they were talking. It was a perverse thrill, I guess! My father told me that I should show humility and always be humble in receiving praise such as the kind the old gentleman had given me.

At the end of the season, we played in two bowl games. Before those games, the entire league had a banquet and invited all the players and parents of all of the teams to this grand hall. It was the banquet room at the Buckner Children's Home—a huge place in the eyes of a thirteen-year-old. There were all of these boys, black, Hispanic, and white sitting around socializing with one another, and it was a beautiful thing to be a part of. This white kid who played on the team that we would oppose in our first bowl game, the Grove Tigers, was calling out some of my teammates at the banquet. He was a brash, cocky guy who played defensive tackle, and his game was intimidation.

Some of the guys on my team came over to the table where my parents and Christie and I sat, enjoying the festive evening. They wanted me to stand up for my teammates and talk this kid down. They were goading me on, wanting me to put this kid in his place. I knew that my father expected more from me, so I just glanced over at him to see his reaction to what my teammates were demanding of me.

Imperceptible to my teammates but very clear to me was the negative shake of my father's head. He would not allow me to be any part of that confrontation. I longed to be with my teammates and stand up to this punk kid who was putting fear into some of my boys, but Pops made the call. I had to sit on my hands. The rest of the banquet was a blur to me. I so wanted to walk up to that kid and let him know that it was on, but I couldn't. It was so painful! The banquet went well, and finally it was over. I needed to get out of there.

As we were leaving, this same cocky kid was also walking out of the building with his father. His dad looked like one of those surly truck drivers with his big stomach and Caterpillar cap. His outward look didn't reflect his inner manner, though. He extended his hand in greeting, and he and my father shook hands. His son, on the other hand, was really getting on my nerves. He told me that I must be scared because I was awfully quiet in the banquet hall. I was seething by this time and I needed to say something—I had to say something! Dad gave me the hand sign to keep my cool. We finally got out of there and made it home. I was miserable. I sat at the kitchen table and asked my father why he would not let me defend my honor and the honor of my teammates.

He looked at me and said, "You will."

The game was a romp. I scored five touchdowns and four extra points—all of our points. Every time I scored, I walked over to that kid and gave him the ball. I only said one thing to him the entire game. Granted I said it over and over again, but it was the same thing. I told him that chickens always squawked! The final insult to all of his banquet ranting and raving was the fact that, after the game, I went and shook his father's hand. His dad told me that I was a class act, and he hoped that some of it rubbed off on his kid! He said that in the presence of his son. I received the game MVP trophy after that and gave it to my dad. Me? Oh yeah, I was walking on air! My father told me never to gloat or try to humiliate anyone. He said that I should be gracious in defeat or victory.

The second game we played, a week later, I hurt my ankle and had to come out for a while. My dad came running down to the sidelines to see if I was all right. He carried me to the bench, and he and the coaches looked at my ankle. I had twisted it trying to make a tackle. I missed the tackle, and the other team scored a touchdown. We were actually losing the game at the time. My coaches were nervous about whether or not I would be able to return. My dad looked me in the eyes and said, "You're okay. Let them wrap it with tape and you get back out there. You have a game to win." I did, they did, and we did. I scored four touchdowns and two extra points. That was all of our points. I gave Pops the game MVP trophy for that contest, too. Afterward I went and shook the hand of my counterpart, the opposing quarterback!

I ran track and played baseball in the spring and summer when I was in junior high school. I ran track for one year and played baseball for three. My dad was at all of my meets and games, and my life was a pretty strict regimen of training for sports and school.

I had to maintain good grades so that I was allowed to play. On occasion, I would slacken up a bit, get lazy, and make a bad grade. I had a close call when I failed the second grading period of a biology course, but my teacher was also the track coach and he somehow managed to overlook the fact that he gave me a failing grade and let me run in the district meet for him. My dad was truly upset with the fact that I failed that grading period, but I was fortunate enough to be able to make it up during the next one. My overall average was a passing grade for the course.

Dad gave me five lashes with his punishment tool for that indiscretion. That's the best way I can describe to you the piece of rubber tube that my father used to whip us with. I say us, but really it was just me. I think Christie had been hit with that thing only once. I think that maybe Debbie and Wanda had been hit with it once or twice, also. I don't think Cathy or Astrid ever got it. I, on the other hand, had felt it several times. It was for those special whipping occasions.

It was a piece of industrial-sized extension cord that had been cut down to about eighteen inches. If it hit you it was like being cut. It only took a few touches from that thing to let you know that you had really incurred my father's wrath. No one else ever experienced the wrath of that thing the way I did. But it was the strongest deterrent ever, and it worked wonders for my dad and me. He was always reinforcing his rule that education was not to be taken lightly!

My father caught me with some pornographic pictures the summer before I started high school. I was fourteen years old and yes, indeed, I was feeling it! I had experienced wet dreams (Dad called them nocturnal emissions), but had never had an orgasm before that. I think the stained laundry was a dead giveaway for us to have that conversation about sex. That conversation shall live within me for as long as I am alive. He didn't attempt to be flowery or anything, he just straight spit it out. It was an uncomfortable scenario for me. The reason it was so bad was because he preceded the conversation about what occurs in a real relationship with a conversation about the baseness and debauchery of pornography and illicit sex.

Having caught me with those pictures, he began to talk in lewd, vulgar street language in explaining their lack of moral and societal values. It was as passionate a speech as one could ever hear about the uselessness of pornography. It made me nauseated, standing there listening to him. But then as suddenly as he was speaking ill of pornography, he began espousing the beauty and sensuality of sex between two loving people. Oh, you talk about a mixed-up kid. I was reeling! He made me and Christie burn all of the pictures from the dirty magazine. He said, "Besides, you're an athlete and you don't need to waste your seed or your energy." That talk made a real impression on me—I think it took me about six or seven days before I looked at another dirty magazine!

As I grew older, I was always glad when each summer was over and school would start—because I seemed to have too much opportunity to meet girls during the spring and summer. Working in a grocery store in the summer was just too tempting for a teenager with raging hormones and a father who was not in the vicinity. Being in school was always a safer place for me. It was structured and insulated to some degree, and it was the least likely place for me to act out. My dad would interrogate me on a regular basis about what I was doing, what was the talk of the dudes my age, and how was I adjusting to living in the civilian community. But I was still running into episodes and encounters with females who really made me want to go against the things that my father taught me.

I felt a lot of pressure from my friends to do mannish things, but I still had the pull of my father working against doing what my friends wanted me to do. Things weren't like I had been accustomed to them being, but I was getting by. Some of the things that were suggested as fun, I just couldn't see the enjoyment in (not to mention some of it was illegal!). Besides, I had to live with my dad; they didn't! He was not coming to get me out of jail for doing something stupid and against the law!

The last time my father gave me a whipping, I was fifteen years old. Christie and I like to joke that it's my "manhood" story. It was the spring of my sophomore year in high school, and I was one of four sophomore Honors students. The others were two white girls and another white boy. The first semester of the year, I maintained a high 3.5 average. The second grading period of the second semester saw my grades plummet to a 3.0 average.

My father saw my report card and some of the teachers' comments did me in. Two "turns homework in late" and one "missing assignments" was all that it took. My father pointed his index finger and told me to get to his room as he was going to whip my ass! I hesitated for a split second and then I went to his room. He told me to put my hands on his cedar chest. He got his punishment tool from under his side of the bed and walked around behind me. He stood there and asked me if I was ready. I told him that I was. After receiving the hardest lick my father has ever hit me with, I spun around and told him that I was not going to take a whipping. His eyes started to bulge as he was just beginning to work himself up to whip me, but he suddenly froze. He stopped and asked me what it was that I had said. I stood up as tall as I could and said that I was not going to take a whipping.

My father smiled at me with the most sinister smile I have ever seen. He put the strap down on his bed and put his hands down by his sides. He took a step back and spread his feet. He put his right hand up until it was at both our eye level and about equal distance between us. He held up that hand with his first three fingers spread apart. He said, "Son, one of three things is going to happen here today. "One," and he dropped his ring finger, "I'm going to whip your ass! "Two," and he dropped his middle finger, "You're going to whip my ass. Or, three," and he dropped his index finger, "One of us is leaving this house right now, and it ain't me." I asked my father how much time I had to pack, and he said I had five minutes. I packed my gym bag and got the hell out of there.

I stayed with my sister Debbie and her family for four days. The incident with my father occurred on a Thursday evening, so I had to go to school from my sister's house the next morning. School let out and I went to work. I stayed with Debbie the entire weekend and went to school on Monday, from her house, again. I went back to her house after school because I didn't have to work that day.

At about seven-thirty that evening, my sister handed me the phone. My mother was on the other line. She told me to come home. Of course, I told her that I didn't think that was a good idea as Pops was still on the warpath. She told me that she wanted me to come home! Again, I had to decline because of the seriousness of the circumstance. My father must have grabbed the phone from my mother because the next thing I knew, he was demanding that I come home, and he didn't sound too happy about having to say that. I asked to speak with my mother again, and she came to the phone. I told her that if there was even the slightest chance that I would have to battle my father about my grades, she needn't waste our time because I was not going to attempt to fight my father, but I absolutely was not going to endure a whipping. She gave me her word, and I went home.

My father always has the last word in his house. He ALWAYS has the last word! I was not into my father's house five feet and he was in my face. He still had that frightening smile on his face. It was a smile that told me that I did not want a piece of him. Never, not even for a nanosecond, did I ever entertain engaging my father in anything physical. Hell, he had hurt me just playing around. I have never been as foolish as my grandmother used to accuse me of being. In fact, thinking about what could have happened to me had I done so makes me shiver now. My mother had brokered a deal with my father that would allow him to choose my punishment and anything was fair game except a whipping. I thought that I could endure anything he dished out, short of that.

Little did I realize to what I had agreed. My father lectured me before he told me what my punishment was to be. He said that while he had to respect the fact that I stood up like a man and made my feelings known, he could not let me get away with not focusing on my studies. He decided that I had to clean up the alley behind our house. I would begin the next day, immediately upon my arrival home from school. I had to change my work schedule or else I would have been doing it in the dark. Yeah, right! I got a friend to take my hours and I arrived home, promptly, from school.

My father arrived home shortly after I did, and we immediately went out into the backyard as he gave me my instructions. We walked out into the alley and he said, "If it doesn't grow, pick it up and put it in the trash." We had an alley that was not paved so there were some overgrown weeds back there. I really didn't see the harshness of his punishment, but I should have. I knew my father well enough to know that I was going to suffer in some way, but for the life of me, I didn't see it coming. In the meantime, my friends had come over to the house to shoot hoops in my backyard. I had a fully-cemented half-court in my backyard, including the lines painted on the cement for the boundary, the lane, and the free-throw line. My spot was a popular place for all of the boys in my neighborhood. It was a regular meeting place for all of us. With the crowd gathering, I was thinking that this cleaning of the alley was going to go pretty smoothly and quickly. I herded all of my friends out into the alley and told them what had to be done before we could shoot basketball.

Of course, anyone could guess what happened next. My father came outside and walked out into the alley where I had all of my friends picking up paper, old baby diapers, milk cartons, cans, old cigarette butts and little pieces of eggshell and everything. Of course, the old man spoiled my groove. He told all of my friends to stop what they were doing and go back inside the fence and shoot baskets. He explained that this was my punishment and that I had to do it by myself. He said that a real man stands on his own and doesn't have innocent people suffer his indiscretions. I nodded to myself and thought, "Good one, good one!" I told the fellas that I would be finished in a few minutes.

My father just smiled. About thirty minutes later, I looked over the alley behind our house and thought that I had done a very thorough job of picking up everything that didn't grow. I figured I still had about forty-five minutes before it would be too dark to play ball. I went into the house and told my father to come look at the alley.

He lifted his eyebrows in surprise and said, "Finished already?"

As we walked out to the alley I cut my eyes at my dad and wondered what was going on in his head. I found out when we got out into the alley.

He said, "Son, what makes you think that you're finished?"

I said, "Dad, I picked up everything that doesn't grow in the alley behind our house, just like you said."

He said, "I guess you misunderstood me; I meant the entire alley behind our **block**, not just our house." He turned around and left, walking toward the house. He looked over his shoulder and said, "Call me when you THINK you're finished."

At about 1:00 a.m. on Wednesday morning, my father came down the alley in his house shoes and white cotton boxers. He had a flashlight, and I saw it crisscrossing the alley as he inspected my work. When he reached me, he asked me how I was doing and I told him I had about thirty-five or forty feet left until I reached the end of our block. He turned around and walked away. He spoke over his shoulder, "Call me when you're finished."

At 2:30 I knocked at the back door of the house which was off of my father's room. He came to the door in his same outfit— his boxers, house shoes, and flashlight. He again escorted me down the alley, crisscrossing it with the flashlight, checking out my work. He spotted microscopic pieces of egg carton and cigarette butt paper along the way and had me pick it up. When we had inspected the entire alley, I was able to come back into my father's house, take a bath, and get into bed. It was 3:45 in the morning.

I was in that alley from 4:45 in the afternoon until 3:45 the next morning. That's eleven hours for anyone who wants to know. I have to smile about that one. I never have recaptured that lost sleep, either. He is the MAN! As for me, I learned not to play with my father's rules! Laughter and tears rule!

I always felt my dad's presence and his absence, even when no one else knew what was going on with me. I remember a football game I played in high school. It wasn't a real game—just a pre-season scrimmage against a school in Richardson, a suburb of Dallas. The scrimmage was on a Saturday morning, and my brother Christie had a scrimmage that morning, as well. It was decided that Mom would take me to my scrimmage and Dad would take Christie. Suddenly, I didn't feel so good!

Christie and my father left the house earlier than my mother and I. My dad was going to drive Christie over to my scrimmage when his was over. Anyhow, Christie didn't realize that I was going to be playing my scrimmage in this new favorite jersey of mine, an old white jersey with a blue number seven on it that my high-school coach had given me the previous year. I had personalized this raggedy old jersey, and it was my favorite jersey to practice in. Everyone else on my team was wearing our actual game jerseys, but I planned to wear my personal one. Christie took my jersey with him to wear under his pads during his scrimmage and when I couldn't find my jersey that morning, I had a cow!

I made like it was a big issue, but I really just wanted my dad to be at my scrimmage and I was looking for any excuse as to why I might not play so well. We got to the playing field and luckily my coach had an extra jersey with him or I would have been stuck. I played in the jersey that my coach gave me, number ten, and for the entire first half of that scrimmage, I played lousy. I mean, I stunk up the place.

At halftime, I went to the stands and told my mom that I was playing so lousy because I didn't have my jersey. It was really because my father wasn't there to watch me and cheer me on. Well, just about that time, my father and Christie drove up and got out of the car. I waved Christie over to me and asked him if he knew what happened to my jersey. He said he had it. I acted like I really needed that jersey, and he would have to go to the car and get it. He ran to the car and got the jersey. It was a bit sweaty but that mattered very little to me. By this time, my coach thought that I had lost my mind. I was standing off, away from the team engaged in this heated conversation with my little brother while he and my teammates looked on in astonishment that I was totally disregarding my coach's plea that I come back to the sideline. I made like I had to have that jersey! I put my jersey on and ran to our sideline just in time to hear my coach say, "Damn it, junior, if you pull another stunt like that, you're not going to quarterback this team." I apologized to my coach and my teammates but tried to convince them that I needed my jersey to perform well. I figured if I couldn't verbalize what the real problem was, I would show them.

In the second half of that scrimmage, I threw four touchdowns and scored twice. My coach said that he would keep an extra number seven jersey in his bag from that day forward, just in case. Little did he know that I would have worn any number he wanted me to wear as long as my Dad was at my game. My father asked me what had happened during the first half of the scrimmage, and my mother decided that she would tell him how poorly I had performed. She went into a rant about how I was not concentrating. How I had called bad audibles, and had thrown into coverages. She let him know that I was stinking up the place. My father asked me what my problem was and I whispered in his ear, "I was waiting for you." He just laughed. He jokingly said that I was totally out of my mind. Later, he told me that being a warrior required having no crutches!

In high school, I attended a school that was racially diverse. There was about an even split of black, Mexican and white kids, as well as teachers. It was a good time in my life, and my father had as much to do with that as I did. I say this because my father trusted me to conduct myself in a responsible manner and as a result, I interacted with my peers of every ethnicity. I had as many Mexican friends and white friends as I did black friends, both male and female. I went places with all of my friends, in small groups or individually, and my father would always bid me a good time with the parting words, "Just ask yourself if you would do it if I was standing there." Those words always kept me from doing anything that would embarrass our name.

I knew that my father and I had totally connected when my father smelled the scent of marijuana on my clothes and didn't have a heart attack or knock me in the head before coolly asking me if I had been smoking pot. I told him that I had not, and he asked me to explain why my clothing smelled of marijuana if I had not been smoking it.

The exchange went something like this: "Boy, your clothes smell like you've been smoking that shit."

I said, "No, I haven't been smoking pot, Dad, but I was in the car with two guys that were. We have a baseball game this evening and I just came home to get my other cleats."

He said, "All right, I trust you to tell me the truth, Son. If you've been smoking that shit, you need to tell me now. If you get arrested for having marijuana, I am not coming to get you out of jail."

I said, "Yes, sir. I haven't been smoking pot, sir."

That was it! That was all he ever said to me, and that was enough.

Playing football my junior and senior years in high school is the most fun and rewarding time I have ever had playing sports. Seeing the look in my father's eyes as he read the newspaper every week and spotted my name in the sports page gave me the greatest joy. I gloried in the fact that I was able to fill him with pride. He said he loved to be in a grocery store or department store, the gas station, or the barber shop, walking around in his military uniform and people would see his name and ask him if he knew me and Christie. He would tell them that he was our father, and they would go into these detailed accounts of the things they saw us do on the football field. I know that nothing made me happier than to see his pride on display as he recounted those stories to us.

My dad has this grin that lights up his entire face and that grin lights up my entire world. My pleasure in playing football was directly linked to that grin. He would arrive to my football games a few minutes late, almost every time. I would look for him while we engaged in pre-game drills and usually he had not arrived yet. We would go back into the locker room just before kickoff and he still may not have made it to the game. When we came out for the opening kickoff, the stands would be so full that I couldn't immediately spot him. I would be keeping my arm warm, throwing passes on the sideline, and suddenly I would hear this booming voice from the stands. It sounded like a foghorn.

"ANTHONY! ALL RIGHT, BOY! YOUR DADDY'S HERE! IT'S TIME TO GO TO WORK."

That was all I was waiting for. It was time to show off for my Pops!

When I was almost seventeen years old, about a month before my senior year was to begin, I was working at the neighborhood grocery store as a package clerk. My mother's long-time employment and association with the grocery chain allowed for four of her children to get their first jobs with the chain. I worked there from the time I was fifteen until well after I was seventeen.

I had been asking my dad for a car for the entire summer, and he finally decided that I was old enough and responsible enough to warrant a car. It was August of 1975 and we went on a hunt for a car that we could afford. I say "we" because Pops had determined that if I wanted a car I would have to be responsible for paying for half of it. We looked all over the city for what he thought was a suitable car for me. I had seen several that I thought were suitable, but he did have the final say in the matter.

I determined pretty early on in the selection process that I was not going to get anything new, fast, or sporty. I was going to get a car that was practical for my needs. I was at an age and of a local stature such that some teenage girls were starting to press me for attention, regardless of my attempts to keep them at bay. I think my father made some decisions that were attempts at making me less appealing to this type of girl because they were moving a lot faster than I was accustomed to. Sex was prevalent in high school during that time, and the Old Man was providing his input into almost everything I did. Girls that I did not even know were calling our house or dropping by unannounced, uninvited, and unknown. My Pops said young ladies were circling me like so many sharks or something.

I laugh about it now, but my father opted for a 1962 Volkswagen Bug as my first car. He was a thoughtful guy, huh? He knew that it was going to be really hard to appeal to girls riding around in that little car. A lot of my friends who had cars had the type that provided an easy, isolated location for behavior my father deemed inappropriate for kids. So it seemed that my little Volkswagen was a perfect solution to preventing me from attracting too many girls. There just weren't many girls that looked at my ride as a make-out mobile.

I think that my father made a lot of decisions like that with the intent of keeping me grounded. He also made me think long and hard about compromising my status in school, in my neighborhood, and in the community.

My Volkswagen was purchased from a private owner at the cost of $600 cash. My father paid it out of his pocket and had me sign an agreement, in writing, to pay him back $25 dollars a week, until I had paid him $300, or half of the cost of the car.

I was earning $1.95 an hour, plus tips, at the grocery store and I was fortunate if I was able to work thirty hours a week. I worked every Monday through Thursday, from 5:30 to 9:30. I was off every Friday during football season. Saturday, I worked eight hours and Sunday I worked six hours. After taxes were taken out of my paycheck, I usually had about forty-three dollars. Twenty-five of that came off the top to Pops and I had to make do with the rest. Money went a long way back then, and I thought I was handling my business well.

The constraints my father laid on me were fair, in my opinion. He let me drive to school, to work, and to my girlfriend's house. In that my life was spent pretty much between those three points, I did not have any problem with my father's rules.

On the Friday nights of our football games, I had to be home at midnight. On school nights I had to be home at 10:30. On Saturday, regardless of what time I got off work, I had to be in my father's house at midnight. The odd Saturday when I got off of work at 6:00 in the evening was about the only window of opportunity that I ever had to be free, moving around in my car without my father knowing my whereabouts. He allowed me that free time, but I always had to make the Saturday night lockdown. On Sunday, I had to be home at 10:00. I missed a lot of wild parties and orgies of the flesh because of those guidelines and curfews. My father taught me that nothing worth having comes free. No, not even freedom!

My father clued me in on so much during that time in my life. I remember him telling me to be careful of the police in Dallas because they liked to target teenaged black boys as troublemakers and make life miserable for some, whenever they could. It was a shock to hear my father speak of authority in such a negative manner. All my life, I had viewed the police as helpful crime fighters on the prowl for criminals and looking to help people in distress. Imagine my emotions when I heard my father speak ill of the police. However, it came to pass that an incident with one of Dallas's finest caused me to understand what my father was talking about.

My close friend and I went to the 7-Eleven one Saturday afternoon. It was on one of those rare occasions when I was scheduled off from work. We had anticipated only being in the store for a moment or two, to buy something cold to drink. In my hurry to run in and then run out of the store, again, I parked my Bug, straddling two parking spaces. I swear to you that my car was the second of two cars in the entire parking lot of the store.

While my friend and I were in the 7-Eleven, we came across one of those video games called Gunfight. We liked to play that game a whole lot and decided to challenge each other. We got carried away and totally disregarded the time such that we were in the store for about fifteen minutes. As fate would have it, a policeman came into the store while we were playing. In a loud, hateful voice he cussed at everyone in the store asking whose car was in the parking lot, illegally taking up two parking spaces. Realizing it was my car, I stepped up and claimed responsibility for the infraction.

That little white officer got in my face like I had robbed a bank or something. He cursed at me, asking me if I didn't know how to park a goddam car. He said that he ought to take my sorry black ass to jail. He ranted and raved as if he had lost his mind and I just stood there, absorbing his insults without making any excuses or trying to avoid responsibility for my actions. I took his abuse like a man and waited for him to finish. By the time he was through, he had worked himself into a frenzy; his eyes bulged and spittle was flying from his mouth like a sprinkler system gone haywire. I stared at him for a brief second and then said, "Sir, I am responsible for the car being parked illegally and I may deserve a ticket for my violation. While you're writing the ticket can I please move my car so that you will no longer be so upset? Also, while you're here, will it be possible to get your full name and badge number? Also, I would like to know the name of your direct supervisor. I think it would do him well to know that you are being abusive in your line of duty, using profane language and making the Police Department look bad. I'm sure that these people here in the store will vouch for your lack of professionalism. You have spent more time cursing at us than it would have taken me to move the car. Do you really expect us to respect you after this? If you do, sir, you are a police officer for the wrong reasons." Having said that, I asked if

I was excused to go and move my car. He mumbled that I could move my car. He did not leave the store until my car was legally parked but he did not give me a ticket. He didn't bother to give me his full name and badge number, either. He also forgot to give me the name of his supervisor. I went back into the 7-Eleven, and several people patted me on the back. My friend and I got out of there soon after. My friend suggested that I had totally lost my mind.

My father taught me how to talk to people like that, though. I tried to conduct myself as Martin Luther King Jr., would have done; assuming the manner of one who stands strong in the eye of the storm. My having role models such as Dr. King and my Pops is something that always gave me courage.

Controlling myself and not being afraid to speak my mind has been something that my father had taught me well. Credit must be given to these teachings, and I give credit to my father for his wisdom in sharing these teachings with me. I know that I have never been arrested or served one day in jail, and the police do not worry me at all.

My senior year in high school, my father caught my girlfriend and me skipping school! My girlfriend was at home sick, and I wanted to see her. I went to school in the morning, but I left at lunchtime and went to her house. I was nursing her back to good health, but parents don't understand that two teenagers could feel that strongly about each other's health. Right!

Anyway, it was about 2:30 in the afternoon and my girlfriend and I were at the Pizza Hut, (nursing her back to health), when who should I see coming toward our table but the First Sergeant. That tingling sensation went down my back because I thought that I was about to be totally embarrassed. He was cool, though. He simply came over to the table, leaned down, and said, "You've got fifteen minutes to get this little girl home, have your car parked in the driveway, and your ass parked in my room. I made it to his room with about forty-five seconds to spare. He said six words. "Put your keys in my dish." I lived a bad stretch with my dad for awhile after that. We didn't speak to one another, and I didn't drive my VW until I got my report card which showed I'd made three A's and one B. That was six weeks later. His laughter and my tears!

My final story reflecting the impact my father had on my life is one with many lessons. It is a story that reflects his influence, his honor, his integrity, and his moral convictions. Were it not for my father, this story could have had a sad ending. If not for his influence this tale would not have turned out to be one of the most amazing, blessed recollections that my family and I have to tell. But my father was the go-to guy, again and he made everything turn out fantastic.

I was home from college for the Christmas holidays during my sophomore year. I was married and had a son, who was not yet two years old. I couldn't work as I was on an athletic scholarship and the NCAA forbade an athlete to work during the academic year. I didn't have much money, and this particular Christmas I was totally dependent on my father's lending me money to shop for presents.

My sister's boyfriend, Otis, and I went to the local mall to shop for the Christmas holiday. Actually, I was just along for the ride. Otis was doing all of the shopping. Anyway, we arrived at the mall and did some window shopping for a while, and Otis purchased a few items for his children. Our last stop was at Sanger Harris Department store. Otis decided that he needed a few ties and hanky sets for his suits.

We must have looked at every silk tie in that store before Otis finally settled on a burgundy tie and hanky and a blue tie and hanky. It was during the Christmas season and the store was packed. The poor young white kid behind the cash register was having a devil of a time trying to check everyone out and keep tabs on the day's receipts that he was in the middle of counting. Otis and I waited our turn and finally we were out of the mall, back in the car on the way to Debbie's house.

We laughed and joked about the stress that young kid at the register was under and both commented we were thankful that we weren't in his shoes. We got back to Debbie's house and went inside to visit and enjoy the holiday season. Otis decided to show everyone what he had purchased and went to get his packages from the bedroom. When he came out of the bedroom, he stood in the middle of the living room and opened his bag.

Unbelievably, he had been given the wrong bag—instead of his purchases, Otis found the cash received for that day's sales in the men's department. There was $3,400 in cash and a few personal checks. All totaled, there was over $5,000 in cash and checks in Otis' bag. He thought he had hit the lottery.

We looked at each other and realized why that kid was so nervous. He was probably trying to keep up with the sack that had all of the money in it while he waited on customers. Needless to say, Otis was okay with the exchange. He was ready to miss out on having the ties for what he now had in the bag. Everyone was thoroughly excited for a little while. Otis even went so far as to make a determination as to how he was going to divide the money. He even offered to give me some of it, since I had been at the store with him.

I thought about taking that money. I thought long and hard. Finally, I decided I didn't want to have any part in keeping that money, and I let Otis know my feelings. He became rather upset with me, as did my sister Debbie and some of our other friends. The discussion became somewhat heated, and feelings got hurt. Otis was a deacon in the church, and I brought to his attention the fact that he would be condoning bad behavior, not to mention that he would be considered a thief if he kept that money.

I asked him if that was the example he wanted to set for his daughters and the other members of the church, who looked up to him. Otis is older than I am, and I was nervous standing up to a grown man, as I was only nineteen. He was about twenty-five at the time. Otis had been a friend of the family for a few years, and he had been to my father's house on several occasions.

My father thought Otis was a fine young man. Otis had shown great respect for my father on any number of occasions, so he thought well of Pops, also. I asked Otis if he thought my father would agree or disagree with us keeping the money. He got quiet and introspective for a moment, and then he said my father would probably expect him to give the money back. I let Otis know that keeping the money or returning it was his decision alone, and that I would have no part in this theft.

Otis's next statement let me know that he at least held my father in high regard. He said that we should call Pops and do what he advised. I felt better just knowing that the decision was going to be put in my father's hands. If he said that Otis should keep the money, then I would gladly partake of the spoils. If he said that Otis should take the money back, the money would be returned. I knew that we were heading back to the mall before I even made the call.

Otis spoke to my father, and shortly thereafter we were on our way back to the mall. Before heading that way, I told Otis to call the store and let them know that they should expect us. The people on the other end of that phone were shocked and amazed that they received this call. They had even begun the process of holding that young courtesy clerk totally responsible, telling him that he was going to have to work and pay back that money. After that his employment was to be terminated.

I am so glad that we called my father! Otis and I arrived back to the mall and, evidently, mall security had been alerted that we were en route. It wasn't five seconds after we walked into the mall that security took up positions in front, behind, and to both sides of us as we walked toward Sanger Harris.

We entered the store and the department manager, the store manager, the courtesy clerk, and a whole host of store security arrived there to greet us at the entrance. They took us back into the offices and thanked us profusely. They even served us some champagne and chocolates that they had for the employee party that they were having after closing.

The first words out of Otis's mouth mentioned a potential reward for our good deed. Of course, the managers were only too willing to give us something for returning the money. They asked Otis what he wanted and he said that he wanted two new suits from their men's department. In the blink of an eye they had written a gift certificate to Otis in the amount of $500. They asked me what I wanted, and I told them that I wanted two things.

They rolled their eyes, expecting some outrageous request. My two wishes were that they not fire the young white kid that had made the mistake of giving us the wrong bag. I told them that he had done the best he could and it was not his fault that he handed Otis the wrong bag. I suggested that they try and fine-tune their closing practice of putting money in a bag that looks just like the bag that you give to customers.

Second, I asked them if they could find it in their hearts to give my little brother a part-time job because he was in high school and needed employment that was flexible enough to accommodate his athletic pursuits. They gave me the application for him to fill out and return to them immediately. A job on the loading docks was his whenever he liked.

I think back and ask myself how did all of these scenes that are my life come to end so happily? Everything I have ever done that has turned out well has done so because I was honoring my father! He has taught me so many of life's lessons and guided me as I learned new ones.

SECTION SIX

A LOVING, LASTING IMPRESSION

I s it possible for a black man to be married for sixty-four years, survive participation in three wars and twenty-six years in the army, retire from the military at forty-four years of age, teach high school kids for twenty-two more years, and retire again? Is it possible that he and his family would travel the world and live in Japan, Europe, and the United States? Is it possible that he could have made so profound an impact in the lives of his children, his grandchildren, and his great-grandchildren? Is it possible that one man can accomplish all of these things and still maintain his dignity, honor, integrity, and humility?

Oh yes, it's possible. I know because my father has done these and many other things. My father is still married to my mother; he did survive three wars and twenty-six years in the United States Army. He did retire from the military, move his family members and himself to Dallas and teach JROTC to high school kids for twenty-two years and retire again.

During this same time, he attended junior college and university at night, for six years. He received an Associate's Degree from Mountain View College and he received his Bachelor of Science Degree from Dallas Baptist University. He and our mother raised seven girls and three boys who have blessed them with thirty-seven grandchildren and thirty-five great-grandchildren. Our father and his lovely wife, our mother, Christine Yvonne Nelms-Laws have been the catalysts for good for my seven sisters, my two brothers, and me all of our lives.

My oldest brother is sixty-four, and my youngest brother is forty-seven. My seven sisters and I all fall between those two in age. Six of my sisters are older than I am and one sister is younger. I am the second son and eighth child of William and Christine. I am fifty years old, and the moral compass in my life is my father. He has set a great example for me to strive to emulate.

He continues to set the example of an honest, humble, intelligent, compassionate, strong, fierce, courageous, proud man. Our father has influenced all of his children with the manner of man he is. I asked my siblings to write down their impressions of our father. I suggested they submit their first and/or fondest memories.

I asked that they share the profound instances of his impact on each of their lives. I suggested that they should say anything they wanted to say about our dad and send it to me for this book.

I did so in hopes that I could use their expressions as additional support for what I know to be the character of our dad. I also wanted to provide an accurate picture of his manner through the years. Providing the impressions of our father, from their hearts and minds, my siblings round my father out so that you know he is a man who wasn't perfect.

He is a man who made mistakes as he grew and matured. He is a man with human frailties. But mostly he is a man of heroic proportions. I hope you can hear the love and reverence for our father that all of us children have always felt.

My father's firstborn, his first son, and his namesake is "the heir apparent to the throne of the kingdom I call home. And where he sits, I know he fits, my Bill!" Those are the first words that I wrote in a poem to my big brother. My big brother Bill has served as a role model for me, all of my life.

I do not think we are as intimate in our relationship as I am with our brother, Christie. I think that this is mainly due to the difference in our ages. He is thirteen years older than I am, and he was a grown man by the time I was old enough to effectively interact with him. I do, however, have fond memories of when he and I did spend time with one another.

He used to pick me up and throw me way up into the air and catch me as I came down. It seemed as if he were tossing me up to the clouds and the funny feeling that I got in my stomach used to take my breath away. He always stood so tall in my eyes. He still does!

My brother Bill wrote:

I am my father's firstborn, and for the first six months of my life I did not see him, as he was in Europe fighting in World War II. My recollections of him are vague shadows and images prior to my fourth year. Somewhere during that year, however, my mother, my sister Patricia, and I joined him in Nara, Japan. He was stationed there at a military reservation called, I believe, Camp Campbell.

Most of my memories of living in Japan with my parents are quite pleasant. We lived in quite picturesque surroundings in the housing area for military personnel and their dependents. We were fortunate in that our family occupied a house that was a standalone, as opposed to many other families who lived in attached multifamily dwellings.

Every day was an adventure, and I remember awakening each morning with keen anticipation and excitement, wondering what the day held in store for my friends and me.

Although the military at that time was segregated, and whites and "colored" people didn't necessarily live next door to each other, still most of my Caucasian friends lived in a housing area that was only shouting distance away.

My best friend was a boy named Jimmy Thompson. We couldn't wait each morning to rendezvous in our favorite spot and share the bacon that our mothers had wrapped in waxed paper for us from that morning's breakfast (yes, Virginia, we actually had bacon practically every morning for breakfast. Imagine that).

My impressions concerning my father are varied, as I would imagine any child's are, depending upon my age. When I was a child around the ages of from four to six, my images of my father vacillated from those of great happiness and love to those of anxiety and a sort of fearful respect.

Although my father (hereinafter referred to as "Dad") did spend some quality time with me, I really longed for more of his attention. Oh, he spent some rather frustrating times teaching me to ride a bicycle, and to do some of the other things that fathers teach their sons, but it seemed to me that he was always doing things that didn't include my sister and me. He was, after all, a young man, and working and having a good time (he was quite a prolific drinker as I recall) were of paramount significance to him, it seemed to me.

During the next stage of my life, between the ages of seven and ten, I can't say that Dad was uninterested in me. But rather there was a great chasm between the sort of time and attention that I longed for and the time and attention he was able to give me. (In later life, I was envious of the time that Dad had for my two brothers, Anthony and Christie. He was retired from the military and was more available for their activities.)

I must say that Dad was always concerned that my sisters, my brothers, and I receive the best education possible. He impressed upon me early on that education was key to success in life. He also inculcated within me a hatred for lying and other forms of dishonesty. Did I ever lie? Did I ever steal?

Yes I did! However, the positive values Dad instilled have served me well over the years. I have submitted some random impressions of my dad.

- *He made great sacrifices on behalf of his family. (He interrupted his college education to return to the military after living in Denver, Colorado, for a time, because he wasn't able to provide for his family adequately while living on the "Economy.")*

- *He risked his life during military conflicts in Germany, Korea, and Vietnam.*

- *He suffered deplorable living conditions in foxholes and sub-zero degree weather, while his family was warm and well-fed at home.*

- *He suffered the indignities of racism at work and the disappointment of being passed over for promotions. (Even as a child, I never took those things lightly and recognized the strength of character that my father possessed.)*

- *He taught me to have a great deal of respect for the women in my life, including my mother, especially; my grandmothers; my aunts; and, of course, my sisters.*

- *He impressed upon me very early in life (around fourth grade) that although sexual intercourse is very pleasurable, a man must always exhibit responsibility for his actions.*

- *He expressed that I should never get so intoxicated that I was not in control of my faculties, and possibly do things that might be dangerous or embarrassing for me or for my family.*

- *He explained to me the mechanics of pleasing one's wife, and that it was an obligation of a man to ensure that his wife was sexually satisfied (even if the effort took all night, and several sessions).*

- *He instilled within me a strong sense of paternal responsibility. (I long ago made up my mind that if I impregnated any female, I would be a responsible father, giving that child the financial and emotional support needed, regardless of how I actually felt about the child's mother.)*

- *He inculcated within me the need to have a good reputation within the community, to be known as a person of integrity.*

- *Because he took great pride in the fact that he had acquired top security clearance during his tenure in military service, he instilled within me the need to always be careful about group affiliations, since bad choices can, and usually will, come back to haunt you.*

- *He impressed upon me the need to be physically clean and well-groomed.*

- *Later in life, he tried to expose me to cultural variety in music, literature, and art.*

- *He made it very clear to me that proper speech can open doors for a black man in today's society. (This has served me extremely well.)*

- *He taught me that what people think about an individual is indeed important, and that first impressions can be lasting.*

I could go on and on, but I won't!

The things our father taught me about life were, of course, taken from his point of view about life, as he knew it. Since I've become an adult, through my study of God's Word, the Bible, I have come to understand a great deal more about what a Christian's viewpoint on life should be, and what is required to worship God in a manner that is pleasing to Him. To be sure, our father gave me the very foundation that allowed me, later in life, to question my own course, and never accept the status quo, but rather to be inquisitive, and investigate the alternatives that life provides. It is this foundation that provided me with an open mind to accept that some things that I had always believed about the universe and the creation were perhaps only partially true, and in some instances, not true at all. It is that foundation that has acted as a springboard to allow me to grow and reach a certain plateau in life from which other vistas can be reached. It is this foundation, provided by our father, that has permitted me to live a more meaningful and productive life now and, hopefully, in the New World to come.

In conclusion, Anthony, I must mention that, in my humble opinion, our father, given where he started, has achieved much during his life! He has limitations, as does everyone, however, the world will never know him as we do. And the world will never know the great and wonderful things that he might have achieved and contributed if he had been born in another time and another place. I love our father! I love you too, Anthony!

Your big brother, Bill
January 2004
William Arthur Laws, Jr.
Human Resources Professional
First child—born on April 6, 1945

My oldest sister, Patricia Yvonne Laws Craig, is the first of our father's seven daughters and the second oldest child in our family. Our father calls her Patti-Mop. Pat has always held a special place in my heart as my "big" sister. She is honored in our family because of her place in the birth order of our father's children.

She has always held to the responsibility of being an example for my younger sisters to follow—one that she proudly, enthusiastically, and honorably maintains to this day. She is a trailblazer! She has been all of her life.

Pat was born feet-first and our grandmother had said that her feet had been leading her all of her life. She has traveled the world extensively, working as a flight attendant for close to thirty years. She has lived in Europe, Japan, and the United States, as a dependent of a career military man. She has been exposed to all the world has to offer and makes a reference to the advantages of having experienced a slice of life in so many different cultures.

My sister Patricia wrote:

I have very fond memories of my growing up. I felt privileged because I had a father whose presence was always felt. I now realize that my being a well-adjusted person comes from the fact that he was a positive presence, as well as a good provider. Because of Dad's being blessed with the strength of character that motivated him to take care of his family's needs, our mother was able to be a stay-at-home mom during all of my formative years.

As I grew up, I began to appreciate my early life and all that I had been exposed to. Of course, the feelings of appreciation grew even more as I matured and realized how much our father must have sacrificed to provide us with the life we had. Prior to that, my good life was just something that I probably took for granted. I know that I had a wonderful childhood.

Traveling as much as we did was an invaluable education all by itself. Experiencing the various cultures of the world broadened my scope of knowledge and understanding of different peoples. Education has always been extremely important to our father and he always impressed upon us the need for and benefit of knowledge.

As we were raised in military installations, we always had the cream of the crop where teachers were concerned. Many American teachers sought the highly-coveted positions of teaching abroad for the government and only the best were afforded an opportunity to do so. We always had teachers who were top-notch in their field.

I can only feel respect and gratitude for the sound emotional, spiritual, and educational foundation provided to me early in my life because of our father's willingness to accept the responsibility as the provider of all our earthly needs. I was constantly nurtured, taught by example, always heard, and lovingly disciplined.

I will forever be eternally grateful for these blessings. Having had this gift of such a wonderful beginning in my life has afforded me the opportunity of being a productive human being. I truly love life and consider each day a gift from Jehovah God. I thank Him every day for my daddy and my mother. These feelings I have expressed come from the depth of my heart!

Patricia
December 2003
Patricia Yvonne Laws Craig
Senior Flight Attendant
Second child—born on February 22, 1947

Pamela Yvette is the third child and second of our father's seven daughters. She has always seemed exotic to me because she was born in Japan. I've always thought that being born there made her ultra-unique as a black woman. During my childhood, Pam always seemed to be the person our dad would leave in charge of ensuring that all of the younger kids did their required chores.

I could have sworn that she was the meanest sister a little kid could possibly have. Now, I realize that she was simply following dad's directives and carrying out her orders. She would have made a good soldier. Pam and I conducted this interview via phone; it was good to hear her thoughts about our father's impact in her life.

Pam is a survivor and someone I would always want in my corner. She is a fierce warrior and always looked out for me when I was young.

Pam said:

My first recollection of Daddy is when I must have been four years old. I say that because I can recall that he and Mother had to come and pick me up from kindergarten in an army jeep one time because I refused to stay in my classroom without my big brother or sister. Of course, Bill and Patti-Mop are older, and they were in the appropriate classrooms for their grade. Naturally, as a four-year-old, I didn't know that and I kept wandering out of my classroom looking for them.

The school administrators called Mother to come and pick me up because I was causing too much of a disturbance in the small school. We didn't have a car at the time so Mother had to call Daddy and see if he could assist her in picking me up. Being in the army, he drove a jeep to our house and picked Mother up, and they both came to the school to get me. I remember thinking that it was fun riding in that army jeep. And I remember that he was driving.

When I was a child, I think that the most profound statement that Daddy ever made to me was that I could do or be anything I wanted to be. He said that girls could do anything that boys could do, and that I should never discount my own abilities and place myself in a relationship with a man who tried to make me feel like I was no one without him. That has seen me through a few tough spots and given me the strength to be independent. The confidence that I learned to have in myself is a direct result of him telling me that when I was a very young child. I believed everything that Daddy told me when I was young. Things don't always turn out like you expect them to, but if you have confidence in yourself and your abilities, I've found that you will survive!

Another dynamic moment in my life with Daddy occurred when I decided to get married instead of going to college. I know that my decision upset him and for the longest time, I didn't think that he was ever going to forgive me for choosing to get married. Hell, thinking back on it now, I should have gone to college. (Pam chuckled when she said that to me.) *Eventually, I think that both he and I overcame our disgruntled feelings about the whole episode and found a common cause to celebrate the path I chose. He has seen all of his grandchildren and great grandchildren, and he knows that they love him dearly. They are my gift to him!*

One thing that I have never doubted in my father is his love for me. He loves all of his children and he made that clearly understood to all who inquired!

I love you, Toadie!
Pamela Yvette Laws Favors—Homemaker
January 2004
Third child—born on December 16, 1949

My sister, Carol Lynn Laws Krause, is our daddy's fourth child. She is the third of seven daughters. She is a registered nurse and works for an international pharmaceutical corporation. Carol and I have shared a love for writing and poetry for as long as I can remember. She used to write poetry and read it to me to see if I could make sense of it. Carol didn't seem so much older and grown up to me even though she is more than seven years older than I am.

When I was in kindergarten and she was in the sixth grade, we rode the same bus to school in the morning and I would always sit with her. She made me feel like I was one of the big kids. She was in junior high school when I was in elementary school so I felt that we were close to being equals. She was always a good mentor and big sister to me.

I have always felt that Carol holds a special place in our father's heart because of several life accomplishments. One of the great memories of my childhood is when Carol won the Miss Black

Staten Island contest in 1970. We drove back to New York from Dallas to attend the pageant and photo session. Our family had pictures that were published in the Staten Island Advance newspaper, and it was a grand affair. I have never seen our father preen like a peacock as he did that day in New York.

Carol speaks warmly about the love our father has always shown for his children. In my opinion, it is a profound statement that a man can make such a lasting impression on his child, so early in that child's life. It is no wonder that a child feels confident and empowered to seek his or her fortune without trepidation.

A father's love protects and encourages. A father's love strengthens and enables. A father's love is never wavering.

Carol wrote:

> I have been asked by my baby brother Anthony to share some significant times in my younger years about my father, William A. Laws, Sr. Anthony asked this of me on November 26, 2003. I assured him I would respond in the time frame he had determined, which was December 13, 2003. Today's date is December 16, 2003, and he has allowed me a reprieve. I believe his humorous approach to my not meeting the deadline is the likely result of something he learned from our parents.
>
> When I was three years old I was the victim of adolescent mischief by a boy who was at least eleven or twelve years of age. I was on the teeter-totter with one of my older siblings. This youngster decided to play a prank and he began to shake the wooden apparatus from side to side. It happened quite quickly, so they tell me, because frankly I do not have any recollection of the fall. The resulting injury included the loss of

several of my upper baby teeth that also penetrated my lower lip. I still bear a visible scar, but my daddy always still called me his "pretty little black baby."

So, if I have no memory of this traumatic event, why have I written about it? Let me tell you what I do remember about that day. I remember being carried by my father into what I believe was a soda shop, or ice cream parlor. I remember having a vanilla milkshake served to me in a tall fluted thick glass. I remember a straw, my first recollection of ever having a beverage from a straw. I remember that for the first time in my little life, I had my father all to myself.

I have a scar to prove that I had this accident, and if not for the scar I would have no knowledge of it. All I have is the memory of being wrapped in the strong secure arms of my father, placed gently into a chair and being spoken to, soothingly, lovingly by my father, my very own daddy.

Lovingly submitted by Carol
December 2003
Carol Lynn Laws Krause
Executive Sales Trainer
Fourth child—born on February 24, 1951

Cathy Marie is our daddy's fifth child. She is the fourth of his seven daughters. Cathy is the most highly educated of our father's children. She has earned her Master's degree in child development. Her nurturing disposition and keen insight about the needs of children have allowed her to make some dynamic observations about the success of our father's role in all of our lives. She points out that children want and need to feel loved, safe, and free to express themselves.

Our father made sure that he did all he could do to ensure those needs were met. In my sister Cathy's tribute to our father, she speaks to his list of positive characteristics and traits—that is, the traits that every man should aspire to achieve in the eyes of his children. His behavior qualifies her success later in her life.

Our father always provided for us, all that we ever needed. He believed in his family, his faith, and his ability. He set the example that all of us follow regarding being responsible for our character, words, and deeds. And again, he always made us feel protected.

Cathy wrote:

A Letter to You, Daddy!

I will always love you. You have been a strong, kind father whom I have always wanted to make proud. You have inspired me to be strong and work hard to get what I have wanted. You have been a good example of ambition. You are clear in loving without judging. You have been and are still a good provider. I have never wanted for anything important and have always known your love is with me.

I will tell anyone who will listen I had a wonderful childhood. I still don't understand hog-head cheese and how it is a food for human consumption. (Smile) I remember you and mother preparing to go to some fancy military function, you in your dress blues military uniform and mother in her evening gown. I remember thinking that the two of you made the most beautiful couple.

I remember the time you returned from war and the excitement and thrill of your arrival. I always tell my students, with pride, that my father is a retired army man. I tell them time and time again that the

*armed forces are what make our nation great. I
remember us singing songs as a family and my thinking,
"We could be the Laws Family Singers and make big
money on stage."*

*The dreams of childhood don't always come
true, but sometimes they do. I live my dream every
day, and I thank you and mother for giving me love,
support, and room to grow that I might realize my
potential. I know that I try to be a good parent because
of the example you set. My children Dirgham and
Kariyma, my husband Douglas, and I thank you and
know that because of you and mother, I am a happy
person. I owe it all to both of you.*

Thank you for being you!
Your daughter, Cathy
December 2003
Cathy Marie Laws Hamilton
Special Education Instructor
Fifth child—born on September 20, 1953

The following is the transcription of the taped monologue of
my sister, Deborah Louise. Debbie, as we call her, is the sixth child of
our father. She is his fifth of seven daughters. Debbie holds an unofficial
position of honor in our family as spokesperson for the "Last Five."
She is the first of our father's last five children.

We have often been referred to as the "Wild Five," as well.
Our father used to claim that he never had the anxiety and stress that
raising his second five children caused when he was raising his first five.
I think that his having retired from the military and us living the civilian
life during our teenage years had an impact on his stress level.

Anyway, I asked Debbie to include her first clear recollection
of him as well as moments or incidents throughout her life when she

felt the impact of our father. During my talk with Debbie she waxed poetic about the strength, wisdom, and character of our father.

We sat down with a bottle of wine and she began to speak freely of her feelings for our dad. She points out how he made her feel loved, protected, and attended to as a child. She also mentions the loneliness and despair felt by our family when our father was away at war. She speaks highly of his influence on her and others. She alludes to his perseverance, and his ability to adapt.

She points out that he was a fair disciplinarian whom she respected and admired. As you read, you will see that she was all-encompassing in her summation of him.

Debbie said:

> *My first recollection of my father is when we lived in Oklahoma in 1962. I was rather sickly, as I recall, and often got nosebleeds for no apparent reason. It was later determined that I was anemic. But what I remember most about that time is that my father would wrap me in a blanket and he and my mother would take me to the hospital.*
>
> *This particular occasion, it was dark and I had to be rushed to the doctor because my nose would not stop bleeding. I remember feeling safe in my father's arms and not very worried about my nosebleed. I remember he told me I was his angel, and that nothing was going to happen to me. At that moment, I had all of my father's attention, and I felt as special as I have ever felt, in my life.*
>
> *Another time I recall vividly is when my father was in Vietnam. It wasn't the same, our not having our daddy at home for Christmas. We didn't go Christmas shopping because my mother had not*

received her allotment check from the army. It seems as if the only thing everyone got for Christmas was a stuffed animal. We were able to get those because we had saved Popsicle coupons and we sent away for those stuffed animals.

That year, we gave them to each other as Christmas presents. A few weeks later our mother received the allotment check and we were able to go shopping. I remember it was a long time before we heard from my father and I became very worried since I knew that he was away fighting a war. I asked my mother if I could write a letter to my daddy in Vietnam. She said that a letter would be fine.

In my letter to my father, I let him know that anyone who is loved as much as I loved him couldn't die in Vietnam. I was ten years old when I wrote him that letter. Two years ago, in 2001, he got that letter out of his strongbox and read it to me. We cried.

I remember hearing the news that my father was wounded while in Vietnam. He received the Purple Heart and Bronze Star for those wounds. I think my letter was prophetic—there was too much love for him to die. I also remember my big brother Bill acting as he thought my father would expect him to, in his absence. He was more mature than I was accustomed to him being. When my father returned home from Vietnam, my world was back to normal again.

I remember that my father had a profound effect on others, and not just his children. Family, friends, and acquaintances were affected by the presence of my father. I remember I liked the younger brother of my big sister's boyfriend. I was thirteen and he was sixteen. I remember kissing him and our young bodies pressing against each other. I got this real funny feeling in my stomach, and I didn't know what was going on. I thought I was in love.

In my youthful enthusiasm, I was ready to let this boy take my virginity and told him as much. He told me that out of respect and admiration for my father, he would not do such a thing to me, my father's daughter. To this day, I appreciate him for that, and I appreciate having a father whose presence influenced the actions of others as well as mine.

When my father retired from the military and we moved to Dallas, Texas, my world changed. Things were not as I was accustomed to them being. We no longer lived on the military base and no longer had that protective barrier surrounding us. Boys were different, attitudes were different, and I was different.

I was a freshman in high school and thought I was grown. My father quickly dispelled that notion as he assured me that I was not as pretty, smart, and grown up as I thought I was or as the boys were telling me. Although I was fourteen and a girl, my father believed in "spare the rod and spoil the child." He was not opposed to taking a strap to any of us, if he felt our behavior warranted as much. He instilled a healthy fear and respect for his authority in all of us.

My father has always been fair but he didn't take too kindly to being tested by any of us. I remember one incident in particular. Our family— all of us that were still under my father's roof, that is—went to the State Fair one Sunday after church. It was Daddy,

Momma, Cathy, Wanda, Anthony, Astrid, Christie, and I.

We had a great time and I remember Daddy saying it was time to go. My sisters and I lingered behind my parents and brothers, walking back to our car. We were busy boy-watching. My father turned around and shouted for us to hurry up, as he was ready to get home and relax. My sisters and I thought nothing much of his insistence that we speed up our pace and defiantly lagged farther and farther behind.

We thought we were too cute to walk too fast and let all of the admiring glances from the interested boys go ignored. My father turned once again and insisted we pick up the pace. He even stated that he would leave us if we were not at the car when he arrived there. I thought nothing of his threat because I knew that my mother would not allow him to leave us. Sure enough, when my sisters and I arrived at the parking lot, my parents and my little brothers were in the car.

Astrid sat up in the front seat of our station wagon with my parents, and the boys were sitting in the far back seat. Cathy, Wanda, and I got into the middle passenger seat of the station wagon, giggling and laughing among ourselves, giddy with the attention we had received from all of the boys we had passed. The car was quiet, and there was an air of tension. My sisters and I didn't know what we were in for.

My father, his eyes bulging and his lips tight in anger, turned to address us. He asked us if we had heard his order that we hurry to the car. We all nodded in confirmation that we had heard him. Evidently, that was the WRONG answer.

Before I could blink, my father had, in one full swing, slapped my sisters and me across all of our faces in rapid succession. It was like being hit by a tidal wave. We sat stunned and silent all the way home. My brothers like to recall that "Dad slapped y'all's hair nappy!" In addition to the physical punishment for disobeying him, he punished us with additional chores at home that day. My sisters and I had to use razor blades and scrape all of the excess dried paint off of the windowpanes of every window in our house. We had to wash them as well.

I remember the jubilation of my little brothers in finding out that we had to do those windows as punishment for our disobedience. That was a chore that they had originally been asked to complete. A word to the wise is, "Do not cross Daddy!" I shall never forget that as long as I live.

When we first moved to Dallas, we lived in a nice three-bedroom, two-car garage, reddish-brown brick home. My dad said that he was renting it with an option to buy it after living in it for a year. Although the house was nice, it was quite a ways from the high school where Daddy was teaching, logistically.

In the summer of 1970, he told us that we were moving to another house. We thought nothing of moving, as we were accustomed to it. Military life had taught us that. It was no big deal—until we saw the house. It was a big house, but it was a wooden frame house that had been in need of repair for what looked like years. My thoughtful, frugal father had purchased it from the owner for mere pennies on the dollar because it required so much work.

When I saw the look on my mother's face I could tell that she was not too pleased with his decision to move his family to that house. I do not know what was said between them, but I thought that our family was going to break apart because my mother was so unhappy living in that house. Whatever was said, my father must have placated my mother with promises of improving the appearance and functionality of the house because it is from that house that the last six of us children launched our adult lives, and where our parents lived for sixteen years.

I must admit, there were extensive repairs made on that house to make it acceptable to our mother. My father always seemed to know what to do in all situations. Lastly, I remember a profound statement my father made to my mother, in the presence of his children.

He told her that she would never have to worry about a stranger knocking at their door claiming that he was their father. He said he would never forsake my mother or his children in that manner. I love my Daddy so much for everything he has sacrificed and done for our family and me.

I love him, I love him, and I love him!
Deborah
December 2003
Deborah Louise Laws Davis—Homemaker
Sixth child—born on September 29, 1955

I spent a day with my sister Wanda Paulette, our father's seventh child. She is the sixth of seven daughters. I visited with her a day earlier and asked her to outline her thoughts about our father so that when I came back the next day, she could just start her monologue about our father without any prompting from me. I would like to commend her on her outstanding contribution to this book.

She expressed herself in such a heartfelt manner that we both became a bit emotional. We have always had a special kinship, sharing the same middle name. We went to school together most of our lives, and have always been able to speak freely with one another about our feelings. People tell us that we look alike. Wanda and I were partners in crime when we were young.

From the time I was about seven, until I was about eleven, my sister and I had friends in common. We were all neighborhood kids of military men, and we all had the same mind-set. We trusted each other with our secrets and always came to one another's defense. Our admiration for our father runs nearly parallel except that she is a woman and I am a man.

Our genders make for a slight difference in degree of focus on a particular strength of our father, but we both strongly agree on the major premise that he is the most revered man in both of our lives.

Wanda said:

My fondest recollection of my father is when we lived at Fort Riley, Kansas. I was nine years old, and I remember my mother telling everyone in the house to come outside and go meet our daddy, who was coming home from Vietnam. I remember seeing a man come up the street with his army duffel bags slung across his shoulder. The closer he got, the more pandemonium began to break out around me.

Everyone was so excited. All of us kids ran down the street to meet my father and we jumped up and down, grabbing at him in jubilation. Everyone was crying tears of great joy, except my mother. She just had this immense smile on her face, and she seemed to suddenly relax. It was so good to have our daddy back home.

I remember when it always seemed that my father was away from home. It seemed that he was either at war or training for war. That was the way our life flowed. We were army brats. We lived on the base, and he was away fighting or training. Christmas was always a grand occasion around our house when our father was home. The Christmas that we celebrated while he was in Vietnam seemed to be one that wasn't going to be so grand.

I always looked forward to that holiday when he was home but when he was gone, I worried that it wouldn't be as enjoyable as it usually was. It's funny the occasions that impact your emotions when you're young. My mother told us that she had no money for Christmas presents because my father's allotment check had not arrived. She did the best that she could, though, giving everyone a dollar to buy a gift for the sibling whose name you drew out of a hat. This was a new kind of Christmas for us because we usually got all of the things we asked Santa Claus to bring us.

My mother explained to us that things would be better when Daddy came home, and we had to make the best of our current situation, for his sake. We had our usual Christmas dinner, but all we could afford to give each other was stuffed animals or a game of some sort as presents. Even though we didn't get all of the toys and clothes and other stuff that we were used to receiving, I felt so much love from my family that day that I believe it was one of the best

Christmases I have ever celebrated. Looking back on that Christmas, I felt the true meaning of the holiday more than at any other time.

Another instance of my father having a profound impact on me dealt with a subject that frightened me, at my young age. I was eight years old and I had a friend whose father, unbeknownst to anyone at the time, was a sexual predator. Back in those days, it was nothing to sit in a male relative's lap or friend of my father's lap and give them a hug. You could usually count on being given some money or a treat from that person. It was something that was viewed as showing love and gladness in seeing them.

It was perceived as perfectly acceptable behavior of little girls and the negative ramifications weren't even considered. My father called me to his room and lectured me about the fact that I was older and that sitting in a man's lap was not suitable behavior for a little girl my age. He said that some men did not see the innocence in that gesture, and bad men would try to do inappropriate things to little girls who did that.

I understood the gist of what he was saying, but I didn't quite understand that there were bad men in the world who would behave toward a child in that manner. I recall being wary of adult males for a while after that. My father did comfort me and assure me that if anybody ever tried or touched me in an inappropriate manner, he would deal with them, straightaway. He made me smile when he said that he would seriously hurt anyone who tried to harm his daughter.

It came to pass that I had a close call with the father of my friend regarding the exact situation my father spoke to me about. I was playing with my friend at her house and her father came home. My mother, in her diligence, called down to my friend's house seconds after her father had asked me to come sit in his lap and give him a hug. I ran out of there as fast as I could, and I never visited my friend's house again. I told her that if she wanted to play with me, she had to come to my house.

Another incident that occurred when I was a child living in Kansas will always be a source of humor to me. I had a little friend who acted older than she really was and did things and said things that I was not totally familiar with. I remember one day she dared me to pull my pants down and poop on the ground, outside the back door of our house.

We had a back porch that extended from the building we lived in, and the corner where the porch met the building was the designated spot for me to do the deed and call her dare. I was unaware that a neighbor who lived behind us was looking out of her window and saw me while I made like an animal and took a dump by the porch.

I thought that it was the most outlandishly daring deed a girl could do, and upon not being immediately discovered, I figured that I had gotten away with it. Little did I know that my mother had received a call from our nosy neighbor and knew of my transgression long before she ever asked me about it.

Later that afternoon, my mother was standing on the back porch and spotted the pile of shit beside it. She asked me if I knew what had happened there. I lied and suggested that maybe a dog had done it. I remember her telling me that dogs did not defecate so uniformly. Disgusting, isn't it?

She suggested that some person had done it, and she wanted to know who would do such a nasty thing. I still feigned ignorance. She was trying to give me an opportunity to confess, but I didn't know that. Finally, after becoming angrier and angrier at my unwillingness to admit my duplicity, she told me what she knew. She pointed to our neighbor's home behind ours.

She said, "You know, the lady across the way saw you pull down your pants and shit outside, don't you?" Of course, I was filled with dread at her next words. "You know I'm going to tell your father when he gets home, don't you?" I was immediately scared shitless! Those were the most dreaded words that my mother could ever utter to any of us when we were kids: "Wait until I tell your father." That was equal to or worse than a death sentence!

Shortness of breath, cold sweats, anxiety, and a sense of foreboding were immediately my emotional and physical symptoms at hearing those words. I did the only thing I could think to do in an attempt to avoid my father's wrath. I went upstairs to my room and took a nap. I thought that maybe this waking nightmare would go away if I went to sleep. It's amazing what you recall of moments in your childhood that impact you for the rest of your life.

I was asleep when my father got home from work. But not for long, though. I guess after kissing my father good evening, the first words out of my mother's mouth had to have been, "Your daughter shit outside and tried to blame it on some poor unsuspecting dog."

All I remember is that when he woke me up, he was still in uniform. I think he may have loosened his tie, but he had not done much else prior to dealing with my misbehavior and me. Daddy's method of punishment worked in three phases. The first was his interrogation.

He asked me the "who, what, when, where, how, and why" of the entire episode. If I continued to play dumb during this part of the process, it would not be a good thing. When he knew the truth, and you knew he knew the truth, there was no need to cause yourself more trouble by continuing to lie or feign ignorance. That just made him totally pissed.

Second, he lectured. He would go into a long, detailed explanation of why he was about to beat you within an inch of your life. He could break the explanation down to your level, regardless of your age, and he made you realize the error of your ways. Usually, by the time he had finished, you were nodding your head in agreement that you needed to be beaten.

The whipping was anticlimatic because he could make you feel so terrible during the lecture. Usually, he would just let you know that he was sorely disappointed in you because he knew that he and our mother had not taught you to behave that way. His disappointment was worse that any number of lashes he could administer. He made you feel so bad about letting him down that you took the lead in insisting on the whipping. He was and still is a dynamic father.

My next recollection of my father's leadership of our family occurred when we moved to New York. Everyone piled into our station wagon. Packed like sardines and pulling a U-Haul trailer, we left Kansas for Miller Army Air Field, Staten Island, New York. The drive wasn't eventful in any negative way. It was an adventure to me!

We took our time driving along the highways of the midwestern and eastern states of this continent, and we had a lot of fun. We pulled over at rest stops regularly and ate cold-cut sandwiches and pork 'n' beans out of the can. We played a lot of silly car games and stopped at a lot of historical marker locations.

I remember when we got to New York, it smelled like sewage and my bigger sisters told me that the odor was the smell of pollution. I didn't know what the word meant, but I know that the air was stinky.

I recall that living in New York was an exciting time for the whole family because our father was not going to have to be away from us anymore. There was a sense of normalcy in all of our lives because our daddy was home every day. With the exception of a few weeks every summer spent on maneuvers, our father was home all of the time. That was a great relief to my mother, as well as all of us children. We all loved it when our father was at the helm. He was our leader, protector, provider, and providence.

I was a preteen and early teenager while we lived in New York. I was in the fifth, sixth, and seventh grades during that time. I can't recall ever being any happier in my childhood than during our three years there. We lived on base and our lives were lived as military dependents. I made friendships and developed relationships that I still maintain today with people that I met during that time. That is the time in my life that my father started raising the bar of his expectation regarding his children.

He took time to talk to all of us about education, maximizing our potential as people and citizens of this country, and not fearing anyone created by God. He challenged us to be competitive but gracious. He challenged us to be aware of our world and all things in it. He challenged us to be creative, thoughtful and benevolent. It was a wonderful time.

I remember one incident that got me into a lot of trouble and warranted a serious whipping from my father. I was eleven years old and a girlfriend of mine suggested that the mailman brought money to people in a yellowish-gold envelope with green paper in it, every month. She suggested that we go into select people's mailboxes and take that money. (The military paid its soldiers once a month in those days)

We didn't know how checks worked and thought that we would find cash in those envelopes. We also didn't realize that every wife in the military knew when to expect her husband's check, and they were always looking out for the mailman on payday. We didn't find money in the envelopes, and in utter disappointment we decided to bury the checks in the ground.

Well, someone saw my friend and me loitering around people's mailboxes. They didn't realize what we were doing at the time, but they put two and two together a few days later, when people started inquiring about their paychecks being late. As usual, my mother got a call, and before too long, I was implicated as being involved in the misdeed.

An actual investigation into the mail tampering resulted in my father being called on the carpet by the base commander and admonished for his inability to control his child. I don't think that my father had ever been more embarrassed. Needless to say, my father personally went to the homes of the soldiers whose paychecks my friend and I had taken and buried, and he apologized for my behavior. He also offered each of them the opportunity to watch him discipline me for my actions. They all declined but stated that they knew that he would do the right thing.

My father was sorely disappointed in me and let me know it in clear, succinct language. I knew that I was going to get a whipping and I dreaded it. More than the whipping, however, I didn't look forward to the lecture I had coming. My father had a rapier-like tongue when he was scolding us, and it hurt more than any physical punishment he could dole out.

Once again, by the time he was finished with his lecture on honesty and morality, lawlessness and brazen theft, the hardships that he endured to make a life for his family, and the sacrifices he willingly made for the safety of his family, community, and this nation, I wished that I could have beaten myself. I didn't have to worry about that, though. He managed that just fine.

One of the behaviors of my father that I have long appreciated is the fact that he did not hold our misdeeds over our heads after he administered his punishment for them. After the interrogation, lecture, and whipping, he was finished with that episode. He had too many children with too many episodes to dwell on one child and one episode for too long. He had a way of addressing an issue, dealing with it, and moving on. He allowed us to move on, as well.

Our father used to make us "kiss and make up." If for any reason one of us was having or had had a run-in with another of our siblings, my father didn't look too kindly on it. He forbade fighting. Whether it was a physical confrontation or words, he did not allow us to have fights with our brothers and sisters, period. If my mother ever mentioned to him that, in his absence, any of us had gotten into it with another, my father would lose his cool.

He said that we could defend ourselves against others, fight for one another against an outsider, fight for our family name, but we were to never fight each other. He would weep in disappointment if he ever heard of any of us fighting each other. Of course, he'd beat the hell out of both parties, but it would upset him to tears to know of his children fighting each other.

Our collective knowledge of that squelched many an angry encounter with our siblings. Whenever an instance of arguing or fighting did occur, if he heard it, you were immediately made to physically kiss and hug whoever it was that you were into it with. The act of doing that always made everyone laugh, even the combatants. It was very difficult to hold a grudge against anyone in my father's house.

My daddy had rules in his house that, as youngsters, we didn't necessarily agree with. He was a fair, just, even-tempered man, but his children did not have very many personal rights, living under his roof. He was always fair about listening to each of us voice our opinion about any subject or concern. We always were given an opportunity to explain our thinking or behavior. But we still knew that regardless of our view on anything, his ruling on our actions was etched in stone. That is the way he operated.

I remember when I was a young teenager and I had written something in my diary. The things that I had written in that diary were my own personal thoughts, feelings, and dreams. I was at an age when I didn't like to talk to my parents about my personal feelings, and it was a kick to feel like I had secret feelings and thoughts that my parents didn't know about. I had written about boys, school, my parents, my siblings, and just all the stuff that a twelve-year-old girl talks about with her friends and feels during that time in her life.

Without my being aware, my father and mother had gotten their hands on my diary and read all of my secrets. I guess one of them caused my parents some angst because my father called me into their room, and he and my mother began questioning me about some of the things that I had written in my diary. Needless to say, I felt like I had been violated. With righteous indignation, I tearfully expressed my feeling that I didn't think their snooping in my diary was fair. As long as I live, I will never forget what my father said to me.

He said, "Fair? Who in the hell told you shit was fair in life? Ain't nothin' in this life fair! This is my house, and you are my child. I will do whatever I feel is necessary to know what is going on with you. The diary is yours to write in, but, dammit, everything in the house belongs to me!" Needless to say, I was crushed.

The ironic part of this story didn't manifest itself until years later and I was the parent. My daughter and sons all went through a phase in their childhood when they stopped talking to me. They were really secretive, and I did not have a clue as to what they were doing outside my household.

As a parent, you want to keep tabs on the mental state of your children so that you can be available to assist them in any way that you can. If they refuse to talk to you or they become secretive in what they are doing, where they are going, and what their interests are, you, as a responsible, concerned parent, have to do everything in your power to find out what is happening in their lives.

If you have to snoop through their closets, dresser drawers, backpacks, purses, wallets, diaries, under their beds, whatever—you do it. Your responsibility is their safety and welfare. I realized that our father was just doing his job when he snooped around in what I thought was my personal stuff.

Another issue that my father is really passionate about is education. To him, it was, is, and shall always be the most important aspect of a child's development. He had always been insistent on us getting good marks in school and paying close attention to what he and my mother taught us.

I think that the most profound aspect of a child's relationship with his or her parents is founded on honesty. If parents are honest with their children, it teaches the child to be honest with the parent. My father was always honest with his children. If he said he was going to do something, he always did it. If he said that he was not going to do something, he did not do it.

He always told us the truth in answer to anything that we asked him. In return, he demanded honesty from each of us. He always said that as long as he knew the truth, he could always provide us with the soundest advice for our problems or concerns. He said that he could protect us if we always told him the truth. He said that he would not defend a liar.

In my life he has always told me the truth, whether or not I wanted to hear it. He also has always been there to assist me with any problem or concern I have had in my entire life. He has let me make mistakes. He has always helped me correct them. He has allowed me to grow. He has enhanced my growth with his wisdom.

He has loved me for all of my life, whether I was going down the left path or the right path; he has been my daddy for as long as I have been alive. I am forty-seven years old, and I still love to call him 'Daddy'!"

December 2003
Wanda Paulette Laws Dodd—Homemaker
Seventh child—born on September 29, 1956

My youngest sister, Astrid, is our father's ninth child. She is the seventh of our father's seven daughters. Astrid has the unfailing spirit of a true entrepreneur. Her confidence in her own abilities is due in no small part to her relationship with our father. She always ensures that he gives her the thumbs-up of approval in her business ventures.

He has always insisted that she could do whatever it is she sets her mind to do. In fact, he has always provided all of us with a vote of confidence in our abilities. He taught us to be competitive and not settle for second best.

In her own words, Astrid communicates that she recalls isolated moments when just she and our father shared a moment that sealed the bond between them. It is those isolated moments that create the foundation of her convictions, inspired by her relationship with our father. Reading her words, you will see the name Warren on several occasions: Warren is Astrid's husband.

Astrid wrote:

>My first recollection of my father was when he came home from Vietnam. I have a vivid memory of that moment because up until that time, I don't remember him at all.

>I was playing outside in the front yard of the Army quarters in Kansas with my baby brother Christie and my older brother Anthony. All of a sudden, my brother Anthony screamed, "Dad!" and began to run down the street. At about that same time, my other older brother and sisters came running out of the house one by one.

>This "Dad" guy was carrying a duffel bag; he seemed to be loved and adored by all of my big sisters and brothers. I remember thinking, well, this is my dad, according to everyone around me, so he must

be okay, and I guess I'm supposed to know him and be happy to see him. I hugged him, but truthfully I didn't know him from Adam.

He didn't seem to be around very often, but I remember receiving presents from my father while he was in Vietnam. I had gotten my ears pierced while we lived in Kansas, but couldn't wear anything in my ears except for 14K gold stems. Periodically Mother would receive earrings in the mail from my father for me. I began to feel a true kinship with him after that.

One time, Mother sent Daddy and me shopping for my Easter dress. We lived in New York on Staten Island. Daddy and I went to Grant's Department Store. He allowed me to pick the dress of my choice. I chose a brown and white polka dot dress, and for the shoes I decided on brown lace-up shoes with a bit of a high heel.

The shoes were a half-size too small, but I convinced him that I would be able to wear them without any trouble at all. When we arrived home, my mother was mortified—brown for Easter and high heels too? I remember her stating, "William, she is only in third grade." I loved that dress and although the shoes did hurt at first, I wore them proudly because Daddy had allowed me to pick my very own outfit. I was so proud and convinced that he must be the best father in the world. After all, he didn't let Mother take my outfit back.

One of my fondest memories is when I received my new bicycle for my tenth birthday. We lived at 2629 Fernwood Avenue in Oak Cliff. It was my birthday, and I wanted a new bicycle in the worst way possible.

I had made my wishes known and was expecting that bike. Well, the day of my birthday finally arrived.

My father came home and said that he was sorry, but he was not able to get the bicycle for me. I told him that was okay and maybe next year I'd get it. Well, to my amazement he had the bicycle in the car. He said that my response had been the correct one and he was testing me. I proved to him that I had character, even in adverse situations.

As the years progressed, I discovered some things about my father that still hold true today. He was honest and sensitive, then, as he is now. He would cry when someone in the family displayed a failure to follow rules and regulations, but he was a strong disciplinarian and that meant he had to show that person that there were certain things that would NOT be tolerated by him.

He once stated to my husband Warren that I was a person who would not be persuaded to do something if I felt strongly against it. He relayed a story about his threatening to give me a spanking if I didn't go up the hill to a friend's house to get my sister Wanda when we lived in Kansas. He recalled how I stated plainly, "I am not going to go to that house and get her," and after several threats of punishment from him, I still refused. He said he then knew that I was strong-willed. He didn't give me a spanking, as I recall, but did say that he would not tolerate disobedience from any of his children. As he, Mother, Warren, and I discussed the incident that morning, I told him I remembered that. I also recalled that at that time, I felt it was dangerous at that house in my five-year-old mind. I can't recall the reason why now.

A pivotal point in my relationship with my father came during a time in my life when I was on a journey of self-discovery. It was 1995, after yet another failed marriage and some voluntary counseling. I went to both my parents and stated that for the better part of my middle and senior high school years, I didn't remember interacting with them very much.

I told them I knew they were busy dealing with some more pressing issues (our sisters), but for some reason, I felt cheated. I felt cheated somehow because I didn't cause a lot of trouble and therefore was left to my own devices and didn't get much attention from them. I especially was hurt when they forgot to even wish me a happy birthday until late into the night on my seventeenth birthday.

As we sat at the kitchen table, they both took one of my hands and said they had come to the same conclusion and for that they were sorry. Such a feeling of peace and healing occurred in that moment. My parents validated my reality and instead of taking a defensive stance, they said they were sorry. From that moment on, I was enabled to spread my wings and fly.

I am no longer afraid of life or being alone. I began to say no when I wanted to and yes when I wanted to, regardless of what others might think of me. I began to make good choices again.

Periodically, Daddy and I have clashed over one thing or another. However, as the years have gone by, we have come to an understanding or a meeting of the minds. I have become more tolerant of human failings, including my own, and he has stated to me, in not so many words, that I don't have to put up with mistreatment from anyone just to please the crowd.

He even once said that I seemed to fall for men who were "too fast" for me. He then said, "You are NOT fast." I realized that he was correct in that assessment, and I have now settled into a very happy marriage with a man who is honest and a strong disciplinarian, just like my Father. Warren is still working on the sensitive part. (Smile)

I love both of my parents dearly, and as I grow older, I realize more and more that they did their job. They took child-rearing seriously and provided me with a sense of stability. I love my life, I love me, but more importantly, I love my father and my mother.

Astrid
December 2003
Astrid Diana Laws Gulley
Promotional Products Agency Owner
Computer Technology Agency Owner
Computer Technology Consultant
Ninth child—born on July 26, 1960

The following comments come from my baby brother, Christie Denique Laws. He is the tenth and final child of our father. Christie is my best friend in the entire world. He is more than a brother to me, if that is possible. He has the same attitude as I do toward our father. We both know that we are men because of our dad.

Christie and I have been as close as two brothers can be without being twins. Although three years, four months, and eight days separate our ages, we were raised as if we were born at the same time. Everything that I experienced as a child, he experienced as well. Once he was old enough to use the bathroom by himself, he was my charge.

We did everything together and we often discussed our father, between just us. We determined that Dad is the best man we have ever known. He has been everything to us that a man can be for his sons. Christie's reflections of our dad bring back wonderful memories of a time in our youth when our father left his mark indelibly on our minds and hearts.

It was the time of our passage to manhood. It was the time when our father began to speak to us like young men and not little boys. It was the time when our dad taught us to stand alone, make decisions for ourselves, and not be afraid of choosing the right thing to do. It was the time in our lives when we began to try to be like him. We both agree that it was a fascinating time in our lives.

Christie wrote:

> *When I was about eleven years old, I played Little League football for a team by the name of the Oak Cliff Cougars. It was my second year on the team. I always had to play with guys that were just a little bit older than me because of my size. The boys that I played with were twelve and thirteen years old, and I was only eleven. I knew all these guys from the neighborhood, but no matter how many times I played with or against them, I still had butterflies competing because I knew that my performance against them was always crucial to the pecking order of our group.*
>
> *Well, one Saturday, late in the season, we were scheduled to play the early night game. The start time for our game was 6:00 p.m. There would be another game played after ours. There were always two games*

played at night, under the lights. All during the late morning and early afternoon of that day, I watched college football on TV.

There they were—my favorite team, the Oklahoma Sooners! That Saturday, a dismal Iowa State University team shouldn't have been allowed on the same field with OU. The score was outrageous—69-6 or 63-0, something like that.

The thing I always noticed most about the black players for OU was that all of them dressed so immaculately in their uniforms. Some wore white shoes, some wore long, thin tube socks, and some wore wristbands that accentuated OU's team colors. Some wore what some football players called spats—not the kind that Al Capone wore but a cool tape job that left the toe and heel of a black cleat in view, while the rest of the shoe was covered in white tape.

To me, this was a seriously cool look! My problem was my cleats were white. They had three black stripes on the side but, alas, they weren't Adidas. Me? I was glad I finally had white cleats. The year before, I'd had some dreary, bubble-toed, cheap, black cleats from a shoe store for men and boys, called Barshops.

It was finally time for me to start getting dressed for my game. It was about 3:30, and I had a sweet idea! I would reverse the look of the tape job that the OU players wore and tape my white shoes with black tape. My exhaustive search for black tape led me to the back porch where my dad kept his tools and supplies for doing handiwork around the house.

I found just what I needed, black electrical tape. As I put on my cleats and the rest of my gear, I kept glancing at the black tape, knowing that it would be just the touch that I needed to help me stand out on the field. Hopefully, my play would help me stand out, as well.

My father had to run an errand and told me that I should be ready to go when he got back. When he returned, I was ready. I had my helmet and shoulder pads sitting on the floor. I had my wristbands on. They had been purchased at the beginning of the season but were still quite white. My mother knew that my brother and I had a thing for wristbands, so she made sure that they were as white as she could possibly get them. Every time she washed them, she bleached them, so they were always extremely white.

And finally, I had on my reverse spats. Black electrical tape covered all of my white cleats except the toe and the heel. Man, I was feeling like a college receiver, only I played tight end! That was a small matter, however, as I had my spats on, and I was going into battle looking fierce. Hey, maybe I could even start a new trend: reverse spats!

Anyway, my dad came in and looked at me to see if I was truly ready. He checked my hair to make sure that it had been combed. I had all of my equipment on except the shoulder pads and the helmet. If you're cool, you don't put them on until after you get to the field.

My dad looked at my jersey. Check. It was free of any and all food particles or stains. He looked at my pants. Check! They were free of stains also, and pristine white from my mother's masterful use of the bleach! He looked at my socks, nice and white and pulled up to the calves.

He looked at my shoes and I knew instantly that something was gravely wrong. Error! Major error! Dad turned a stern face down to me and said, "Boy, get that shit off your shoes. Quit trying to be a show-off and be thankful for the talent you have. Oh, and please tell me that you didn't waste my electrical tape wrappin' your damn shoes up like that."

My father was terribly disappointed in me. Needless to say, I was crushed—I mean, totally humiliated! As I somberly sat back on my bed to take off my reverse spats, Anthony came into the room. I began sobbing, uncontrollably. He tried to console me but to no avail. He did help me remove the electrical tape, though.

Not even thinking that I would have to take the tape off so soon, I didn't realize the damage I had done to my cleats. They were now speckled with the tape's adhesive residue from midtoe to midheel. They looked awful!

I listlessly made my way to the car, trudging along like a pirate walking the plank. I soon noticed that dust particles, dead grass, leaves and everything were sticking to my cleats. I felt horrible! I now looked just like a slow, plodding tight end! I cried some more—rather quietly this time, though. Mind you, my dad wasn't at all for the sniffling. My tears fell silently, all the way to the football field.

I got out of the car and went over to the spot where our coach told us to meet prior to pregame warm-ups. I didn't look at my dad while we were warming up. Hell, I was mad at him; I didn't want to look at him. Besides, I was afraid to look at him after so obviously disappointing him. Warm-ups were over, and the game started.

We had a really good team, and we beat our opponent decisively that day. I had a fantasy-type game: four receptions, two for touchdowns, and 170 yards receiving. I also had all of the gook, dust, grass, and foreign particles that electronic tape residue on white cleats could possibly attract.

On my two long touchdown catches, my dad ran with me. He was on the sideline and I was on the field. As I sprinted toward the end zone, he was the only one that could keep up with me. Before I could even give the ball to the referee, he scooped me up into his arms, my feet totally off of the ground, and he kissed my helmet right where my cheek would be had the helmet been off.

He did that on both of my long touchdown catches. Now, mind you, I was an eleven-year-old boy, and my dad met me in the end zone with hugs and kisses and praise. Not what most boys would want happening in front of a crowd, I would surmise. Well, for me, it was beautiful and it still touches me to this day, realizing that my father knew that I didn't need the spats.

He knew that I didn't need the Adidas. He knew that I didn't need any of that fluff and brand-name stuff to be good. He taught me that to be good, I had to work hard and practice, practice, practice—that is, if I wanted to be the best that I possibly could! Later, after the game, he took me to the ice-cream parlor where he let me order the biggest ice cream cone that they made: a five-scooper!

Later that year, when I played for my elementary school basketball team, everyone on the team had Converse basketball shoes—except me. I had white Converse knockoffs. The shoe had certain parts molded to look like Converse, but cost considerably less, at about $3.99 versus the $10.99 for real Cons.

Well, needless to say, my father's lesson stuck with me for the rest of that year and the rest of my life. I discovered that I didn't need Converse All-Stars to play basketball well. I don't think anyone even noticed my shoes as I received my trophy at the annual awards assembly. I had been voted Most Valuable Player on our city championship basketball team. I love you, Dad! You will always be a shining example and my hero!"

"Judge ye not the warrior by the gleam of his armor, but by the glint in his eye!"   Anonymous

Christie
December 2003
Christie Denique Laws
Promotional advertising sales executive
Tenth child—born on January 9, 1962

As I read through each of the letters and transcripts containing the feelings of my brothers and sisters, I was not surprised to discover that the underlying theme to all of their impressions is love, guidance, and protection. Clearly, that is what a child carries as a lasting memory of growing up with his or her father. Unfortunately, how many of our children are growing up without the gift of those impressions of their fathers?

SECTION SEVEN

---•---

AS THE TWIG IS BENT SO GROWS THE TREE

While my name doesn't have a *Dr.* in front of it or a *PhD* behind it, my life qualifies me to have an opinion. I am also educated and very mindful of the historical journey that black people have made. With what I have experienced in my life and the stories about their lives that my parents and grandparents told to me, I have a sense for what life must have been like for a black man during the early part of the twentieth century. It fascinated me to think about it when I was young and as I have grown older.

I think that too many young black children haven't been made aware of what blacks have suffered long and hard to gain because these children have not had someone to remind them of the history of that suffering. From a historical perspective, many of them haven't been fortunate enough to interact with a positive male role model. Sadly, not nearly enough have had that positive male role model as their fathers.

I know that everyone lives a different life. I know that quite possibly my childhood with my father is too ideal to believe. Maybe I was shielded from all of the harshness and disillusionments that so many young black boys have experienced. Maybe I am lucky to have been born when I was.

I often reflect back on my childhood and realize that I did not experience too many instances of tragedy or sorrow. My first experience of feeling loss was at the funeral of my grandfather. My dad's father died when I was fourteen and that was the first time I ever felt sorrow. Because he died of natural causes, his passing was deemed a "homegoing," and it was a celebration rather than a tragic situation. A "blessing" was how all of my adult relatives insisted we view his death.

My brother and I often sit and reflect back on how we felt during our childhood and how it has affected us today. We both feel deeply grateful for the benefit of having had our father in our lives as children. We've both found that his presence and guidance in raising us have helped us in our relationships with our sons.

Have you ever paid close attention to the statements of some of our country's most popular black icons, both the athletes and the celebrities? Many of them have acknowledged, or the media has informed us, that only their mothers raised them. I have observed that many of them, males and females, heap all the praise for their success on their mothers without even mentioning their fathers.

Has the role of "black father" and "positive male role model" in our community been so greatly compromised that it no longer serves a purpose in our children's development? Have black men been so negligent that we have become a nonfactor in the development of the next generation? Who is going to teach black boys how to be respected, responsible men?

It is not an exaggeration to suggest that some black men haven't accepted the responsibility of nurturing their children. I am concerned that if too many black men continue to neglect their children, the generations to follow will be missing a vital part of what makes them emotionally whole and well rounded.

Emotional outbursts and mood swings, group or club association, drawing attention by manner and dress, fancy coiffures, and glittering jewelry are all mannerisms and behaviors that we associate with women. This is not the manner or behavior historically associated with masculinity. Now it has become the manner of young men, but there is a dangerous twist to it—and that twist is violence.

Where does it originate? More than likely in communities with no history of positive male role models present. Likely, it occurs in homes that are missing a strong, positive, male influence. Children are taught the roles they are to assume, and the manner that they emulate is a result of who and what they see.

Fatherless upbringings profoundly affect the emotional disposition of a child. For many of our young black men, missing out on the emotional connection that occurs between a father and his son is shown in some of their behaviors. In 1985, I wrote a poem trying to express what I thought it might be like—the difference between having and not having a father.

Just Being a Man...

If the answer were quite simple, and the question near the same
Could black boys know the method; or for matter, make the claim?
Could they hold the torch of legacy and assume their rightful posts,
As the sons of their proud fathers and the subject of his boasts?
What of the case for sons of fathers, who cannot make the claim
Of knowing their fathers' whereabouts? They didn't get his name?
They did not get their father's love, his guidance or his strength.
They search, in vain, for validity, and go to damaging lengths.

What challenges their premise that their mother is their guide?
She's their bridge on troubled water and will never leave their side?
How can they be sufficient in their skills, their prep for living,
If they don't know how to wean themselves, the net that she keeps giving?

Their mothers, they can't show them, for a woman is not a man.
As if they knew the formula, by now they'd loose their hands.
And tell them they must stand alone and blaze a path themselves.
They'd pray for them like all moms do, and wish for them life's wealth.
Their fathers surely would teach them that life's a series of tests.
Instill in them integrity, and insist that they try their best.

They'd love them tough, the way Dads do, and monitor their ways,
They'd show them how to cautiously walk and extend for them, their days.
So might then the situation be, for many young black men lost,
That being a man requires payment, and they don't know the cost.
Their mothers don't know it; their father didn't show it and they have cried too long,
Small wonder they're mad, and deep down, sad—their life is a forlorn song.

Something that saddens me is the fact that while black men are some of the best athletes and entertainers this world will ever see, many of them have fathers who have never played a role in their lives. The media will highlight the glorious and graceful athletic feats of some young black athlete, and his father is not present to share the moment with him. The man that begat the superstar is nowhere in that star's life and something is missing. The connection that is the soul of a warrior is not attached, and something is missing. A conscious effort must be made by that athlete to disregard the hollow feeling that is the connection that is missing with that father.

A child is two halves making one whole. He is a part of his mother's bloodline, and he is a part of his father's bloodline. He receives his spirit from both sets of his parents' genes. He longs to share his success with his father, the man he should respect most, aspire to emulate, and strive to make proud. One of my best friends in this world was a great athlete, and he was sad not to have had his father see his athletic exploits. I would imagine to have never experienced that feeling is everlastingly painful. I still hurt for my friend!

My brother and I often go to Little League and high school athletic events throughout the city to watch all of the dynamic young athletes we see; there is an apparent shortage of men in attendance. There are always extended families of mothers, siblings, aunts, and cousins present. Often, we even see older gentlemen, quite obviously too old to be fathers, but surely grandfathers or uncles. But there seems to be a shortage of fathers at these events. Our young athletes need their fathers' support, as well as their mothers'!

Hip-hop music, the voice of a new generation of an injured oppressed minority, has been vilified and labeled as antisocial and dangerous. But those labels couldn't be further from the truth. Hip-hop music is the missing father for so many of its generation, such that it is now embraced across the entire nation. All you have to do is listen to the words. And I beseech you to listen!

Listen to some of the sorrow-filled, angry words that overlay the beat of hip-hop music and know that it represents much that is missing from the lives of too many of our black youth. What is the origin of those words that are on the lips of too many black children these days? Those words are not born in a happy home!

Those words are a language born of the despair and fear of not feeling protected, guided, or loved. It is that boastful, vulgar language that masks a fear so intense that anger is the result of not being able to shake it. It is the language of the depressed, despondent, and disheartened. It is the language of the street!

No one speaks lovingly to anyone they care about in this manner. Do lovers refer to each other in this manner these days? Do parents speak to their children in this manner these days? I hope and pray not. What message is being conveyed, and what does it mean for black society?

Suddenly, we have softened our stance that we will not be referred to as anything other than the respectful, thoughtful, courageous people that we have fought to be. Too many of us declare that we are fine with and accepting of all the derogatory names, caricatures, and images that we fought for four hundred years to overcome. What used to pass as derogatory has now become the chosen reference our youth trumpets as cool and hip.

I can recall, as a child, the shame and anger in being called a nigger. I fought white kids who tried to associate those references and labels with me. Now, black children and even young black adults speak this negativity as if it were honorable. Honorable, that is, as long as it is a reference made by us, about us!

Look deeper into the origins of the words our younger generation chooses to use and glorify. The word gangster is defined as a member of a criminal group. Our children are proudly labeling themselves as criminals, and none of them even realize that they have assigned themselves to a life of conduct outside of the law. It is no small wonder that society at large is hesitant to view young black men as capable of assuming a productive role in our society. Not to mention that the ethnic groups that the term was historically used to describe, preyed on our community in the past, inundating it with illicit drugs, racketeering, and murder. We should be proud to refer to ourselves as gangsters?

What of the word pimp? Historically, our community looked upon that individual as the lowest type of man we could ever identify. A pimp was a man so absent of morals that he was willing to exert his physical dominance and control over our fairer sex and abuse and malign her physical weakness because he was lazy, ignorant and too sorry to make a life for himself. Sure, he would promise a woman his protection, but at what cost to her dignity and emotional well-being? Have young black men chosen to disrespect the young women of our community to such an extent? When did we decide to leave moral conduct out of the equation that is part and parcel of the lessons we teach our children? Aren't too many black youngsters suffering enough loss of dignity by society at large, for us to condone our children's use of that word to describe their status?

Whore, 'ho' or hoochie is so implicitly demeaning that I should not have to elaborate on the definition. Unfortunately, many use it so commonly to describe the supposed manner and/or behavior of a particular type of woman that it doesn't even faze our community anymore. Nowadays, it is used to simply refer to any female, and we should be ashamed by that. How can we insist that our larger society treat us with respect if we will not even respect ourselves? Too many would suggest that it is not meant to be harmful or mean and vindictive, but surely we can see the damage it is doing, can't we?

I remember when I was a youngster of eight years old, and I made the egregious error of giving my big sister the "finger." I was too young to know what it meant and had no real idea of its implication. I had just always observed my older siblings exchanging the quiet insult at one another on occasion and thought it to be an antic of older, wiser kids. Well, my sister pitched a glass of ice water at me, and my high-pitched squeal disturbed my parents as they watched television.

My father called me into the living room and asked why I was making so much noise. I thought nothing of telling him that my sister had tossed cold water on me. When he asked me what I had done to warrant her behavior, I innocently showed him what I had done. He whipped me like I was a criminal! He demanded that I apologize to my sister (who, by the way, was in tears for getting me into trouble). I did not know what transgression I had committed until he told me after he finished administering that mauling, and you can bet that I refrained from doing it ever again!

I often hear young children spew expletives in a manner that is more than just upsetting—it is deplorable. What has become of the punishment of washing out the mouth of a child heard to utter "cuss" words? Again, what are we allowing our children to become? Is no one concerned about this behavior? When we were teenagers, my father used to speak to my brother and me about the inappropriateness of profanity in the presence of adults and females. He relented regarding the conversations that boys will have among themselves, but he always said that there is a time and place for all behaviors. He referred to it as "locker room talk amongst the fellas" and identified when that kind of language was allowable. He made it clear that it was not necessarily condoned, but, as boys, we should expect to hear some of it within the confines of an all-male setting.

Last, what pride or satisfaction should any of us take in being referred to as a "playa"? Is a fast-talking con man, a dishonest and disloyal individual now a celebrated icon in our community? May I ask on whom is the game really being played? Who are we subjecting to the games being played? Sure, in the short term, we may be able to pull the wool over the eyes of society at large—but in the long run, who is losing the game?

What has become of the proud black fathers who would not tolerate such vulgar, derogatory language in their homes? What are we allowing to transpire in our community? Whatever happened to the days when a child feared the consequences of his father's wrath? Alas, many children do not know their fathers; we are losing the ground that four hundred years of suffering and fighting against oppression has allowed us to gain.

It seems that we are paying a greater price for the freedom bought with the pain, suffering, and sacrifice of our forefathers and elders than we had thought.

Look at some of the attire of the icons of the hip-hop movement and ask yourselves, "Would a proud, black father allow his daughter to parade around in public in some of the clothes young girls wear nowadays? Would he turn his eyes away from the trousers falling off the butt and hips of his son? Would he permit the message that it conveys?

Must we pattern our style of dress after convicts in prison clothes? That is the origin of the "sag" or "baggy" look. Black people died so that we could hold our heads up high and present ourselves as well-groomed, dignified individuals. That was a difficult time, an unforgiving place, and a premium cost paid in full. We should not have to present ourselves as if we are cast members in a vaudeville performance anymore. I wonder at our (supposed) progress!

In 1984, I felt despair for what was happening to my Oak Cliff community right before my eyes. Healthy people were trying to fool the system—get welfare and Section 8 housing. Drugs and violence were controlling the community, and sexually-transmitted diseases were becoming more and more rampant. In my despair, I wrote this poem:

Just Thinkin'!

You know what? I've been to a lot of different places and seen a lot of sights.

I've pressed for days and days and I've sat up deep into nights.

I've prided myself in my ability to reason; to make sense of conflicting views,

And not let myself be easily swayed by opinions or what's on the news.

But lately I'm thoroughly puzzled by the mind-set of the masses.

No one wants to pay the cost or participate in all of life's classes.

What ever happened to our willingness to try, to put forth the effort and time?

Why does such an inordinate amount think they're entitled? It's a crime!

I was thinking yesterday, about years past. The dead, they would wonder, "For what?"

To realize the Dream some blood was spilled but doors opened that had been shut.

And Harriet would say to some of us now, "I guess my effort 'twas vain."

Martin would cry, "Why the hell did I die," if amongst us we still inflict pain.

The men of today are wont to be weak; don't want to compete, or can't.

The women, they rave; it's money they crave and readily they will rant.

"What have you done lately?" It's on everyone's lips. The quality dips and slips.

"They holdin' me down." Offered up with a frown, as he stands on the corner and sips.

My father told me; taught me all sorts of lessons and insisted I never forget.

My mother showed me; I watched her every day. I'm as good as any woman I've met at cleanin', at cookin', at laundry, and shoppin'. I am fine all by myself.

Someone who loves me and I in return just merely enhances my wealth.

So you see, I've been thinking and my heart is sinking; haven't we learned anything?

We'd as soon fight our brother and serve someone other, than let the freedom bell ring.

I love where I am, and I will be damned if you think that I'll take a step back.

Our lineage is strong; we must not prolong our return to Martin's dream and that's a fact!

Stereotypical portrayals of black men by the media would have the world and ourselves believe that if we are not athletes, celebrities, or gangsters, we are nothing. Some young black people are inclined to think that nothing in life is more important than the amount of easy money one can make, the labeled clothes one wears, and the fancy car one drives. Pops taught me at a very early age that it was my responsibility to earn whatever it was that I wanted. I wrote this poem shortly after recalling a conversation I had with my dad about his reluctance to easily consent when I asked him if I could use his car to drive my girlfriend home. He let me know that her safety and welfare was my responsibility, not his.

Everybody Ain't . . . !

Been around for awhile, seen a lot of mistakes.

In thinking and behavior, the decisions one makes.

And I can't help saying what the problem might be,

Wanting something for nothing. Nothing worthwhile is ever free!

I will always remember what my Old Man said.

When I asked him for the car and he shook his head . . .

He said, "Damn, Son, everybody ain't gonna drive my car.

Everybody, 'cause they want to, ain't gonna be no star.

Everybody ain't gonna have all they want to eat.

Everybody ain't gonna wear good shoes on they feet.

Everybody ain't gonna get to be the captain of the team.

Everybody ain't gonna get to realize they dream.

Everybody ain't gonna have nice new clothes that fit.

Everybody ain't gonna get rich and have a lot of shit.

What I'm sayin' Son, is this, so hear what I say—

You bust your ass for what you want, and get it the right way!

Our jails are filled with young black men who repeated the same mistakes that young black men before them had made. Numerous studies have shown that the majority of today's black youth serving time did not live with their fathers. In some instances, the father was also serving time in prison. Who is available to teach our sons how to avoid the pitfalls of trouble and the misery of prison?

In the late '70s, I was in college majoring in sociology. I had the opportunity to visit the Texas Department of Corrections' for one of my classes. We were attempting to identify the dynamics of what caused criminal behavior and assess the criminal system. Our assignment was to interview individuals and try to determine the cause and effect of their antisocial or criminal disposition. We were also trying to gauge the degree of rehabilitation that the different facilities presented.

My class visited a detention facility that housed male juvenile defenders, and I was saddened at the hardened faces of the young detainees I saw there. We were allowed to speak with them but we could not ask them what their last name was nor could we talk to them about their cases. It was an eye-opening experience.

It was also a frightening experience because I was a sophomore in college and only nineteen years old. What was so frightening was the fact that some of those detainees were only a year or two younger than I was, and to hear how far off of the lawful path they had strayed at such a tender age was appalling. I asked my professor if I could speak with some of the detainees about their childhood and he told me that I could.

I asked a young black teenager if he could tell me when he first started thinking about behaving in the manner that led him to being jailed. He said that he was about nine years old when he first got into trouble with the authorities. I asked him if he ever considered what his behavior was doing to his mother and his father and that is when this young, hardened, juvenile softened and became somewhat withdrawn.

I tried to let him know that I was not passing judgment on him, but that I just wanted to know if possibly his childhood had any bearing on his current situation. His story will replay itself over and over in my head for as long as I live. He said that he never knew his father, and his mother was just a teenager when he was born. He said he was left alone with his brother and sister during the evening and nighttime because his mother had to work to feed their family.

He remembered always being afraid because he was the oldest child home, and he worried that something would happen and he would not know what to do. He liked getting into trouble when he was young because someone would have to pay attention to him when he was in trouble. As he got older, he began to go out after dark and look into people's houses. He remembered that he got mad because he saw kids sitting around watching television and laughing with their mothers and fathers, and he had never had a chance to experience that. He said that he started targeting those kids as his victims. He would beat them up whenever he crossed their paths.

Eventually, his aggressiveness grew to the point that he began going into people's homes and just wrecking them. He would be crying the entire time that he was damaging these homes because they all had things in them that his home didn't have. I asked him if he could tell me how he felt justified in damaging other people's homes, and he made the most amazing, chilling remark.

He said, "Fuck it, they got a daddy! He'll just keep working and replace all of the stuff that I broke. Sometime, I think about killing some kid's daddy just so that he'll know what it feels like not to have one." He then smiled and said, "Then, I'll be his friend!"

I didn't even try to explain to him that his thought process wasn't healthy because I was totally afraid of this seventeen-year-old boy. I tried to put myself in his position and asked myself how I might feel in that same circumstance, but I couldn't even begin to comprehend what it must have been like to be home alone and afraid of every noise or shadow. I couldn't imagine not having my father in my life. I couldn't imagine ever becoming that angry, but then again, I had never walked in this young man's shoes.

Another visit my class made was to the state's minimum-security facility in Fort Worth. It was there that I engaged a young adult black woman, twenty-five years of age, in a conversation about her situation. Again, I was instructed by my professor to refrain from asking what her last name was and what her case was about.

Apparently, she had gotten mixed up in a drug bust, but I couldn't really get into the details of her incarceration, and I had to ask her to stop talking to me about it. I just wanted to know about her childhood and again try and determine if her early life had directly impacted her adult behavior. Her story, while not nearly as frightening to me as that of the young male juvenile's, was still just as sad. Hers was a distressing situation that supported my premise that a fatherless childhood directly impacts a person's life.

Her father had abandoned their family when she was very young, and she could not remember him ever being in her life. She had never met him during her childhood because her mother would not let him see his children. She said that her mother was a religious woman and that she was often at odds with her mother's strict rule. As she grew older, she felt that her father probably abandoned them because of her mother's overzealous religious behavior.

She said that when she was a young girl she would have dreams that her father had come back into her life. She always felt disturbed after the dreams because, in her dreams, her father did not have a face. She did not know him!

The young woman said that her mother's sister, her aunt, had a loving marriage and family situation, and she always wondered what her life would have been like had she been born to her aunt instead. Her cousins would tease her when she was young because she did not have a father.

She entered into a sexual relationship with an older boy when she was fourteen years old, and she became pregnant as a result. Her mother would not allow her to live at home and keep her child, so she left. Her older boyfriend would not have anything to do with her after their child was born, and she ended up living with her grandmother.

Her grandmother assumed the role of mother to her child and she was free to do as she wanted. Over the course of four or five years, she found herself a willing participant in a small drug ring. Her career of criminal activity landed her in prison.

I asked her if she felt that she would have been in her same situation if her father had been at home and her answer was gut-wrenching. She said that because she never remembered her father and did not know what kind of man he was, how could she say that her life would have been any different or better? She said that she surely would have liked to experience the possibility, though. I asked her if her child's father ever made any effort to be a part of their child's life, and she said that her child had never seen his real father. She said that her eleven-year-old child called her grandmother's boyfriend "Daddy"! Black children dream of a life with their father. Unfortunately for this young woman as well as her child, the dream did not turn out to be their reality.

Our final visit during our assessment of the penal system found us in a maximum-security facility. The black inmate population was 60 percent of the total population of the facility at that time. It nauseated me to see so many black men caged like animals. I wondered if there was a working correlation between the suffering of our black community and the presence of all these men here instead of in the community providing love, guidance, and protection to our children.

A more sickening realization was that the prison was a walled city, totally self-contained with men assuming all the roles within it: men who prey on other men, men who welcomed the attention of other men, and men who witnessed it all and despaired because of what they had seen. We were not allowed to talk to any of these incarcerated souls, and I am glad. I had become depressed by the complete and utter lack of pride and hope that I had seen there and did not wish to interact with any of those men. Their behavior, the lewdness of their words and manner, the posture that they assumed—it all haunts me still.

During the middle '80s and early '90s, I worked at an expensive private psychiatric hospital. It was nationally known as one of the top five psychiatric facilities in the United States. My eyes were opened to a lot of our society's woes during that time. My employment there allowed me to see the world from a different perspective.

The hospital had about 120 beds for patients and a staff of about three times that amount. The hospital had a twenty-four-bed unit for adolescent and teenaged patients and it was filled to capacity with white children, ages eleven to seventeen, mostly girls. There was one black female child on that unit and she was the child of a wealthy black family.

A friend and a co-worker of mine at the time also had a part-time job with the city's forty-eight-bed MHMR Juvenile Detention Center; the center was filled to capacity with young black and Hispanic children aged thirteen to eighteen, 85 percent of whom were boys. Both facilities assisted children with mental and emotional problems. The difference in the two facilities that served the same purpose was that the psychiatric hospital was like a college campus and the detention facility was like a prison.

In talking about his other job, my friend said that most of his detainees didn't have a father that played a role in the child's life. He said that in his conversations with some of his charges, they often expressed anger at not having a father's presence in their lives.

He said that those young black boys often felt abandoned by the absence of their fathers, and they felt that the world had neglected them. They were angry, unhappy, and lost—and our solution to their inappropriate behavior was incarceration and medication.

These young boys felt deep resentment at being relegated to the locked doors and the high fences that surrounded their home. Their resentment was acted out in destructive behavior. Fights that ended with some young black or Hispanic boy having his head slammed against a wall and cracked open or someone getting stabbed with a fork or sharpened table knife were regular occurrences at the detention center.

I was told that some of those kids were sent there because their mothers could not control them. It was not always the case that they had engaged in delinquent behavior but that they had become too big for their mothers to handle. They acted out and behaved inappropriately at home, and they were sent to the detention center as a result.

The mother hopes that the county can supervise her manchild better than she could on her own. Rather than enduring the hardship and uncertainty of successfully raising that child by herself, she hopes that maybe the county can succeed. The detention center is a reflection of what has been and continues to be missing in the lives of some of our children. Fatherhood has been missing in some of the homes of our black community for too long!

I have seen the fork in the road that can make or break a young man's life and I know of too many young black men who took the wrong fork. The overwhelming majority of them did not have a father to guide them the way mine guided me. Unfortunately, history can't be changed and it will take another Herculean effort, just like the fight for freedom, to disseminate the knowledge of our fathers and their fathers before them, so that we can be whole again.

We can't neglect the issue of our young teenaged daughters looking for love and happiness at such an early age. It must be emphasized that she is not capable of nurturing a relationship or a child of her own, and neither is the object of her young infatuation. It is happening to an alarmingly high percentage of young women in our community.

What about the issue of some of our young black men fathering offspring that they do not step up and claim as their own? Their mind-set is that impregnating a young black girl is a symbol of manhood, and a badge of honor is to have multiple "baby's mommas" throughout the city. Their behavior is as if their ill-conceived intent is to populate the community and this nation with little black children who will perpetuate the cycle of despair that these young men, themselves, dreamed of overcoming. It is a double-edged sword created in part by the lack of love, guidance and protection that a missing father could have provided them, but isn't and wasn't present to do so.

Why does our community ignore history and not heed the warning that the past affords us? In 1985, I wrote a poem questioning whether or not we black parents are providing the proper guidance for our children. It presents a scenario that is too prevalent, even more so today, than when I wrote it.

Predetermined Destiny?

Father, was that you reflected in his eyes
Or was his vision chemically impaired?
Was your failing related to his demise?
Was he acting as you would not have dared?
Mother, do you hear your daughter crying?
Fearful of facing young motherhood alone?
Should she have withstood the heat of assuming?
As a juvenile is often prone?
Father, is your presence commonplace
and your call a resounding warning?
Does your black princess, attired in lace,
cower at your parental scorning?
Mother, do you show him that you are a lady
and clarify your son's masculinity?
Do you capitulate that a real woman's not shady?

and there is beauty in his own femininity?
Parents, are our children emotionally secure?
Are outside influences defined and categorized?
By them, will all challenges be met?
Or, is their destiny not to be recognized?

Left alone and unprotected, some black women and children of our community make the best of a tough, tragic situation. The absence of the father as the head of his household, for whatever reason, has driven some black women to resort to extreme measures to ensure that their children are provided for and protected. Often, in her attempts to do all that she must to make a life and home for her children, she forfeits the time and energy needed to maternally nurture them.

In many cases, the streets are the fathers of some of our young black men. The streets that casually gobble up young black men like so much human fodder for despair's cannon. Why is the percentage of good black men thought to be so small, even by those of us who know that there are still some honorable black men out there?

The reason is because there is a large percentage of black men who have failed our families! As black men, we must recommit ourselves to standing up and assuming our rightful roles as men in our community. We must give our women back their femininity and allow them to concentrate on providing the maternal nurturing that is needed by our children so that they can effectively assume their roles as law-abiding, productive citizens of the world.

The struggle that has been hard-fought and continues to exist should have us better prepared to provide our children with the knowledge and tools to realize that we can accomplish any and all things. Where are our black leaders, and what posture do they assume?

Historically, how many black fathers just suddenly didn't come home one day, during the middle and late decades of the twentieth century? How many generations of a family have felt the void of not having had a man in the household? Think about the numerous ways that the black community has lost its men during these times.

Black men have fought in every war during the twentieth century, and too many died. Black men have been and still are the victims of racist violence, and too many have died. Black men have been and still are victims of the proliferation of drugs in our society, and too many have died. Black men have been and still are the victims of the gang mentality, and too many have died. Black men have been and still are victims of society's woes, and too many have died.

Has the loss been balanced? The fact is that it hasn't been balanced for a long time now. Where are the fathers of many of the outstanding athletes we see on television every day? Why are so many women having children without being in a committed relationship? Where is the real example of fatherhood being presented? Who is showing little black boys how to be strong black men?

I have been to a lot of different places, and I've seen varied cultural differences. I've done some pretty exciting things in my life, and I've enjoyed meeting the people whose paths crossed mine. I've attended the inaugural balls of presidents and I have hobnobbed with celebrities. I've vacationed in Barcelona and the Spanish Isles. I've hung out in Cozumel, Mexico; Montego Bay, Jamaica; and in Vail, Colorado. I've partied in Hollywood, Las Vegas, and London.

I've jumped from airplanes and I've rappelled from helicopters. I've experienced love and war, and they both fascinate and confuse me. I've played football with and against some of the best athletes in the world. In college, my team was composed of future All-Conference, All-American, and All-Pro athletes. In fact, one of my former college teammates is in the National Football's Hall of Fame! However, know that for me, there is absolutely nothing that can compare with the feelings of pride, excitement, and exhilaration that comes from being a true father and daddy. Any healthy male can impregnate a female, but only a real man gets to be a father and earn the right to be called Daddy.

I composed this poem in 1984 to celebrate my love for my sons. They were seven and five years old at the time. Being around them and watching them grow gave me the most joy of anything that I have ever had the privilege of experiencing. Their smiles, hugs, questions and antics caused a love in my heart that is so overwhelming that I can not see how any man could not want to experience it. It is one of the many feelings in my soul that I am certain is a gift from the Master!

Four Shining Eyes

Four shining eyes, two disarming smiles
Two pairs of legs that run for miles.
Two mischievous wonders so full of fun.
They are my world. They are my sons!

Two questioning minds, four testing hands,
That touch to know and ask to understand.
Two eager apprentices when work's to be done,
My inquisitive students, my aspiring sons!

Two shiny backsides that paddle, I must
Two showers of love from clouds of trust
Two small investments that return a ton
My now, my future, my wonderful sons!

Two beautiful little people, mine 'til I die.
I watch them grow and have to sigh.
Their mother and I are the lucky ones
Blessed by the Master with beautiful sons!

My sons make me proud to be their father and proud that they look to me for guidance. That means I have done my job. I have done my job in protecting them until they reached manhood, and I have been and will continue to be the first person they can come to for guidance. They have made me proud in their accomplishments, and they have made me proud of the manner in which they carry themselves.

The oldest of my sons held down a job at the same insurance company for several years while going to college. He attended school at night after working eight hours every day. He has held jobs in his field of study, Computer Technology, since graduating in 2004. My youngest son has two degrees and graduated from college in 2002. He has been employed in the Marketing/Advertising arena for the last seven years. At thirty-two and thirty years of age, they are a part of the future of our society. They love hip-hop music, but they are not hoodlums. They love women but they are not married. Nor do they have any children. They love sports, but that is not the center of their awareness. They recognize the pitfalls and hardship that are synonymous with being a black man in our society. They are handling their business just as I have taught them. Society should not mistake them for something they are not!

The final section of this book is not an indictment against black men. In fact, I know that many of us are trying our damnedest to compete in this society that has been stacked against black people, and we are holding our own. But we have work to do, and I hope that I have stirred the souls of some of my brothers. I also want to celebrate those who have raised and continue to raise their children. They are to be recognized and respected because life is still a jungle and someone has to walk point!

My prayer is that those of us who have accepted our blessing as fathers, daddies, and role models will maintain. Also, it is my desire that those of us who have not might yet strive to assume the honorable position as real fathers and daddies to our children. It is going to take the same willpower and courage that it took for the good black men who have gone before us. We are indebted to them, and we must not let them down.

No one said that life is easy. I think that each and every one of us knows that a relationship between a man and a woman is not guaranteed and may not stand the test of time. But one thing is certain, and that is the need for responsibility and commitment in providing a stable life for our children. Stability is the springboard for every child's success. Each and every one of our children deserves an opportunity to succeed. Being a real, good father is something that all men should seek to achieve, and, thereby, provide stability for their children. In our community, it is essential to our survival!

There are more opportunities in life than a child could ever dream. Black fathers and black mothers, just as all other fathers and mothers, are accountable for the parameters of their children's dreams. Let us assume our role as the launching pad that allows our children to dream without boundaries.

My parents allowed me to dream without boundaries! My father is still doing what he has done for me all my life, and I am fifty years old. He is setting the only example I have ever needed to see: to be a proud man and a good father. He has shown and continues to show me how to handle my business. He has shown and continues to show me the moral conviction, integrity, and honesty that make him the good man that he is. He has loved me unconditionally. He has always been my hero. And as for me, I will continue to try and live my life so that he and my sons will be proud of the man that I have become.

I have learned to be a father from my father!